Minot Judson Savage, William Henry Savage

Belief in God

An Examination of some Fundamental Theistic Problems

Minot Judson Savage, William Henry Savage

Belief in God

An Examination of some Fundamental Theistic Problems

ISBN/EAN: 9783743417717

Manufactured in Europe, USA, Canada, Australia, Japa

Cover: Foto ©Lupo / pixelio.de

Manufactured and distributed by brebook publishing software (www.brebook.com)

Minot Judson Savage, William Henry Savage

Belief in God

BELIEF IN GOD:

AN EXAMINATION OF SOME FUNDAMENTAL THEISTIC PROBLEMS.

BY

M. J. SAVAGE.

TO WHICH IS ADDED AN ADDRESS ON

THE INTELLECTUAL BASIS OF FAITH

BY

W. H. SAVAGE.

SECOND EDITION.

BOSTON:
GEORGE H. ELLIS, 141 FRANKLIN STREET.
1881.

COPYRIGHT,
1881,
BY GEORGE H. ELLIS.

Transfer
Engineers School Liby.
June 29, 1931

Dedication.

Believing that the true way of escape from the "Slough of Despond"
is by *going straight through it* to the other side, like "Christian,"
and not by *crawling back* to the starting point, abject
and mud-spattered, like "Pliable," the
author dedicates this book

TO

THOSE WHO AGREE WITH HIM IN THIS OPINION.

CONTENTS.

		PAGE
I.	Preface	11
II.	Origin and Development of the Idea of God	13
III.	Does God Exist?	30
IV.	Can We Know God?	47
V.	Is God Conscious, Personal, and Good?	65
VI.	Why Does not God Reveal Himself?	82
VII.	Shall We Worship God?	99
VIII.	Shall We Pray to God?	118
IX.	The Glory and the Shame of Atheism	137
X.	The Intellectual Basis of Faith. By W. H. Savage	153

PREFACE.

IF a book does not commend itself by meeting a want and accomplishing a work, there is little use in an explanatory preface as a defence against either the public or the critics. In the present state of the public mind on the subject of Theism, no apology for speaking is required from him who honestly thinks he has anything to say. Whether the speaking has been to any useful purpose, the audience itself must decide. The author ventures to believe, however, that, both as to method and result, he has something to offer that is not merely an echo of what has already been said. Believing "the scientific method" the only one by which truth is to be attained, the attempt has been made to avoid all assumption. And if all the following positions cannot be scientifically demonstrated, it is believed that, at any rate, nothing is yet known that can contradict them. The term, scientific method, is of course used in its broadest sense, as including the observation, orderly arrangement, and verification of all known truth. No one has the right to narrow it down to anything less inclusive.

The following eight chapters are only eight Sunday morning discourses, delivered in the regular order of the author's work. But, judging by their reception as thus given, he dares to hope they may be of use to some beyond the limits of his usual congregation. It is perhaps proper to say that, with two exceptions, they have never been written, but are published from the stenographer's reports.

The author takes the liberty of calling special attention to the address by his brother. He believes its method to be new, its treatment fresh, and its argument unanswerable.

BOSTON, Feb. 23, 1881.

WHERE IS GOD?

"Oh, where is the sea?" the fishes cried,
    As they swam the crystal clearness through;
"We've heard from of old of the ocean's tide,
    And we long to look on the waters blue.
The wise ones speak of an infinite sea:
Oh, who can tell us if such there be?"

The lark flew up in the morning bright,
    And sung and balanced on sunny wings;
And this was its song: — "I see the light,
    I look on a world of beautiful things;
But, flying and singing everywhere,
In vain I have searched to find the air."

Origin and Development of the Idea of God.

THERE was a time in the infantile life of Shakespeare before a conscious thought had passed through his brain. There was also a time when he waked up to this wonderful thing that we call consciousness, though as yet he was a child and thought as a child. His ideas were crude and illogical, and to a grown-up man foundationless and foolish. His utterance was stammering, or meaningless prattle. But there came a time when this same Shakespeare's brain blossomed out into the white lily of a Cordelia, and bloomed into the blood-red horror of Lady Macbeth. What is true of an individual is, in a parallel sense, true of a race. There was a time before the human race had ever thought of that which to-day fills the universe and absorbs the profound attention of man. There was again a time when this human race, in some crude, childish, stammering, prattling way, first began to think God and try to say God, to give utterance, expression, to this new and magnificent idea,— this idea which in the later ages has blossomed out into the magnificence, the grandeur, the purity, the self-sacrifice of such men as Buddha and Jesus. What we want to do at the outset is, if we can, to get back to the birth-time, or as near to it as possible, of this first human thought of God.

Modern knowledge, within the last fifty years, for the first time in the history of the race, has kindled a light at which we may set on fire our torch; and, with this torch in our hand, we may trace back the path of human progress along and down toward the primeval twilight before the sun was up; even beyond the twilight into the darkness of the yet sunless night where only a few stars even cast their pale and trembling rays. With our torch, we may go down and back into the crypts and caverns whence sprung the fountains of this great river of human life, whose waves have been the rise and fall of empires, and whose frothy, foaming crests have been dynasties; between and beneath which has flowed, in dark and sullen strength, all the common life of the race. With this torch in hand, then, this morning, let us go back and catch a glimpse, if we can, of the earliest form of human worship. What will it be like?

A father or chief of a tribe has died. After long waiting to see if this departed life is not to return and take possession of the body again, they have done what they can to protect this body from decay. For they said, in accordance with reasons which I shall very soon give you, "Perhaps he has only gone away for a little while. He may come again to-morrow or next week or next month, and want the body again. We will keep it, if we can." But, having become tired with waiting, they have buried the body,— preserved as well as possible,— away out of sight; they have built over it a mound, a tumulus, a grave; and on this grave they have kindled a fire to guide the departed spirit in the night and on its journey. They bring here and place upon this grave — the first altar — food, offerings of food, for the dead. They bring flowers, they bring tobacco, weapons, whatever they conceive the departed chieftain cares for, whatever he loved in his life. And here,— mark you, the origin of human sacrifice,— if he was a bloody, powerful chief, thirsting for the lives of his enemies, slaughtering during that life as many as possible, they bring to the grave the captured members of the clans that were his old-time enemies, and put them to death at his tomb, as being the sweetest offering they can bring him, that which will bestow upon him the highest degree of satisfaction. And then some appointed orator of the family or the tribe stands up, and in the noblest language he can command rehearses the characteristics and the grand deeds of the dead; or, forming in procession, they march around the grave, chanting in rude but rhythmic utterances verses of eulogy for the departed. Here is the first hymn of worship that the human race ever sang. Here, then, is a picture in brief outline, yet clear enough, I think, to be distinctly understood, of the earliest form of worship known to man,—the worship of the father or the chief of a tribe.

But now, as we look upon this scene, there springs up and looks us in the face the fundamental problem of all: How did it happen that these people supposed that this chief was not extinct? He speaks no more, he no longer moves hand or foot, no longer exhibits emotion or passion, no longer cares for food or drink, no longer opens his eyes. How does it happen that they believe then that he is not dead, that he lives somewhere and cares for something still? You must not be surprised if the reasons that I offer you for the birth of this belief seem to you somewhat slight and trivial. You must rather divest your minds of the results of ages of study and thought and culture so far as you may, and get back to the utter, perfect simplicity of children, ignorant of all the laws of the world. And then you will have to be able to understand the processes of their reasoning. For according to the light they had, according to the experiences through which they had passed, they reasoned as logically and as well as we can to-day. What do we find? Why, here is one of these men walking along in the sunshine, and he sees his shadow by his side upon the ground, and he says, What is this? He knows nothing of what is so commonplace and familiar to us to-day, the law of the shining of light that compels any opaque substance to cast a shadow. He knows nothing of all this. He does not look up into the heavens; and, when a cloud passes over the sun and the shadow disappears, he simply wonders where it has gone. He looks over into the water, and there is his reflection in the stream or lake or pond; and he wonders what this other self means. When he goes away, that also goes away. It puzzles him. He tries to explain it; and the explanation that he gives is that this is a shadowy duplicate of himself, that is alive as he is, that is capable of coming and going at will as he comes and goes. And this is the most rational explanation that he can make. And this belief has been transmitted down the ages, and remains a part of the popular myth and story of the world. Perhaps you will remember the story of Peter Schlemil, who permanently lost his shadow, so that he wandered through the world all the rest of his life with this spiritual, second self detached and gone. This shows how this belief ingrained itself in the thought of man.

Then another thing helped him to believe in this duplicate spiritual self. He laid down and fell asleep; he knew nothing about the origin or philosophy of dreams: indeed, we know very little about them, even to-day. But, while he is lying here asleep, he is off on a journey; he hunts, he fights, he converses with his friends; and, strangest of all, he meets there and talks face to face with the shadows of those that have long been dead. And this, to his thinking, is just as real an experience as any that he has when he is wide-awake. He sees there in his dream the shadowy dog, the shadowy antelope, the shadowy horse, the shadowy bear, the shadowy weapon, the shadowy kitchen utensil of his camp; and he believes that there is another world than this that he sees with his eyes open,— there is a shadowy world, a duplicate of this. And by and by, when he wakes up, he finds himself lying just where he fell asleep. And his interpretation — a natural and logical one on the basis of all he knew — was that this shadowy self which had been out on an excursion, hunting or fighting or visiting friends, had come back again; and, when it came back and entered into the body, the body awoke, and he sees now the world from which he started.

We carry still in our common, every-day speech the traces of this old belief. Suppose one of your number should faint this morning and be carried out into the vestibule. You watch over her, you sprinkle her forehead with water, you chafe her hands, and look for signs of returning consciousness; and, when she opens her eyes, you say, "She is coming to." Finish the sentence, and you have the belief of the ancient world,— "She is coming to herself again." The spirit has been away, and the body was unconscious. The spirit returns, and the body rouses itself.

Here, then, is the origin of this primeval faith of man, of the universal belief in the continued existence of the life after death. For they reasoned — and they reasoned well, when they said — the spirit of the body of the man that was asleep stayed away a little while and came back. Another was in a trance, or in some combat he was smitten with a blow upon the head that made him unconscious, perhaps for hours or days. The spirit is away all this while. It comes back again after a long time. It is able, then, to live without the body, one day, two days, a week. Why not forever? It perhaps will come back after a thousand years, and take the old body again. In this way, and as naturally as ever sprung a grass-blade out of the earth, grew up the belief in this other duplicate world.

And then this connected itself again quite as naturally with the early beliefs in regard to the place where the dead lived, the location of this other world. Tribes, from one cause or another, migrated from their old homes. They were at the mouth of a river, and they wandered up its banks and made them a new home; or they were driven across a mountain chain; or they lived, to escape cold and wild beasts, in caves and dens, and then, growing stronger, dared to come out into the sunlight and make themselves a place of abode beneath the blue skies. What more natural than for them to do precisely what we are doing all the time,— idealize our old homes, idealize the past, make it more beautiful than the present, forget all the ills that we suffered then, remember all the ills that we suffer now, and so create a contrast between the golden past and the iron age of to-day. This followed, and out of this soil blossomed their dreams of Edens and golden ages and beautiful homes in the past. And they believed that the dead spirit did what was the most natural thing in the world,— went back to the old home. You will find, for example, tribes to-day who have migrated up some river-bottom, who, when they bury their dead, put them in a boat, and set them afloat on the stream, that they may go back home. We find that they believed that they returned to this resting-place of their race, over the mountains, or back into the caves. And out of these caves, the primeval homes of men, have been developed the beliefs in the underground Hebrew Sheol, the Greek and Roman

Hades, the Underworld of the nations. Or, as they saw far off toward the sunset and over the sea cloud islands, glimpses of what seemed to them supernatural and beautiful lands, there sprung up in their minds a belief that the dead had gone toward the sunset, as Hiawatha did, floating along that stream of light adown the west, seeking for the "Islands of the Blest." Thus out of these perfectly natural human experiences sprung these phases of human belief which, in some form or another, have existed until to-day and have dominated the world.

The first worship, then, I have said, was the worship of ancestors, the worship of the dead fathers of the tribe. And you will see very easily that these gods would become good or bad, great or small, according to the characteristics which they displayed during their earthly career. And, after they were dead, they became the kings of the underworld, where they waited to receive the followers and members of the tribe.

Out of this belief in ancestor worship sprung, first, fetichism. What is fetichism? It is the worship of a stick or stone or tree or any inanimate thing. How did it happen that men ever became so irrational as this? You must not attribute to them so little reason or sense as to suppose they really worshipped a stick or a stone. Some accidental connection sprung up that led them to attribute to this tree or to this stone or to this stick a piece of good luck or a piece of bad luck. And they believed, as I have already intimated to you, that the stick and the stone and the tree and the mountain and the horse and the dog all had a second, duplicate, spiritual self. They believed that these were repositories and sources of mysterious power. Or they believed that they might even be the temporary abodes of their own dead ancestors and friends. For it was a part of this belief that the spirit could go out and come back; and that any other spirit could also enter in while the first was out, and take possession, as a man might enter an empty house. Thus even more than one might make it their common abode. We find Mary Magdalen in the New Testament represented as a home where seven devils abode at once. And another had so many that he called his name legion, for he said we are a great number living here together. They then would come to worship this stick or stone or weapon so accidentally linked with a piece of good or bad fortune; in the one case praising it for the good, in the other attempting to please and placate it, to ward off the bad.

Then the next step in the development of gods was the worship of animals, of mountains, rivers, trees, stars, the sun and the moon. How did this come about? By a double process. In the first place, as I have already explained in regard to fetich worship, they believed that these had a spiritual duplicate self. And a like belief existed clear down to the time of the great astronomer Kepler, just a little while before Newton; for Kepler himself believed that every star had a ruling spirit which controlled its movements. That was the most rational method he could then devise to explain the regularity of their journeying through the heavens. And the other process by which this came about was this: You know it is common even to-day, and it always has been, for prominent men in barbarous tribes to take some curious or symbolical name. We find, for example, at the West, Sitting Bull, for one of our Indian chiefs. We have Black Hawk, we have The Great Crow, we have The Eagle; we have those who take as a name the tortoise or the hare or the beaver. After a time, the people would forget that this was a symbolical name of a man. And, being accustomed to say that a beaver or the sun or a star or a mountain was the ancestor of their tribe, the worship of sun or star or moon or mountain itself would spring up as naturally as a seed grows from the ground where it is planted.

And then this, of course, would lead us naturally to the next step, to the development of polytheism, the worship of a multitude of gods, good, bad, and indifferent, high and low, great and small, all over the world. There are to-day in India alone thousands of gods worshipped by the common people; thousands in China. There were hundreds in the Pantheon of Rome. The whole universe, by this terrific imagination of the early mind, was peopled with figures and spirits, grand or grotesque, hateful or kindly, possessed of all the different characteristics that they discovered in their own multifarious life.

And then what followed next? Two forces as natural as the dawn were at work in the midst of these multitudinous gods of polytheism. One was the power of natural selection by which some of the gods were lifted up into greatness, and others were cast down to a lower rank, or even into obscurity and forgetfulness. You can see how natural it would be. Egypt becomes a great country, of which her neighbor nations are afraid. Of course, then, the gods of Egypt are mightier than the gods of the petty tribes about her. Babylon spreads her wings all over the East. Her gods are as grand in their majesty as are her kings upon earth. And so there would naturally spring up, as there sprung up great kings and great despots, great gods; while others would become small and feeble. By this process, Jupiter became the king of all the Olympians. And so among the Hindoos, they had there one who was first and supreme. And so in China, so all over the world where this progress of thought went on.

And, along with this process of dividing the gods into two

ranks as great and small, there went on another process of dividing them according to character, as good or bad, as friendly or hostile. But they worshipped both just the same. For you can very easily see that, if we really believe that there is a power outside of us who can harm us, we shall try to keep on the right side of him, if he is malignant, just as earnestly as we shall try to please and rejoice in him, if he is kind. And this process of thought has not died out yet. I have had occasion to tell you of an intelligent lady in Boston with whom I have talked within the last two years, who said to me: "I would like above all things to believe as you do, but I do not dare to. I do not know but there may be a god in the heavens like him of whom I have been taught; and, if there is, I am afraid of him." Only a little while ago a Christian mother in England was found teaching her child to bow whenever the Devil's name was mentioned; and as she explained it to the woman who asked her about it — "Because I think it is safer," "Give the Devil his due." Keep on the right side of any power that may help or hinder. Thus I say this process went on dividing the gods into good and bad.

Another process, very curious and yet that you will see is very natural, was going on at the same time. A great nation conquers some other nation, gets it under its feet. The gods of the conquered nation are supposed also to be conquered and partake of the degradation of the conquest; so they are relegated to a lower sphere. When Zoroaster taught his new religion and converted hundreds and thousands of the people to his new faith, the gods of the Hindoos, the religion that was conquered and driven out, became the malignant sprites and devils of the Parsis. And this has left its imprint in our very language; for, did you know it, the word "deity" is derived from the old Hindoo word "deva," and the word "devil" is derived from the same. Deity and devil originally were one, divided at last by the process and development of human thought that made one class of forces and powers good and another evil. And so we find all through the nations of the past that they have worshipped every force and power of nature. They worship the bright sky, and they worship the storm-cloud. They worship the sun as a life-giving, beneficent power; they worship the sun as the scorching, burning flame of Moloch, the blasting breath that makes the deserts and withers the crops. Thus, in their worship, they had two classes of gods, light and dark, good and evil, hateful and helpful in their natures.

What is the next step beyond polytheism? For these gods could not live and multiply themselves to human thought forever. It is what Professor Max Müller calls by a word that may be unfamiliar to you, henotheism. The next step beyond polytheism is not monotheism, it is henotheism. What is that? It is worship on the part of some people of one god exclusively, but without the accompanying denial of the real existence of other gods. To illustrate what I mean take the case of the ancient Hebrews. We are accustomed to speak of them as monotheists. They were not monotheists, they were henotheists. They believed that they ought to worship Jehovah, their god; but it never entered the heads of the common people to deny or even doubt the existence of Dagon, the god of the Philistines, or the gods of the Egyptians, or the gods of Tyre and Sidon, or the gods of the Moabites. They believed they existed, believed they were real gods: only Jehovah was their God, and they must worship him and him alone. You will find traces of this all along in Hebrew thought. Recall, for example, such a familiar phrase as "King of kings and Lord of lords." Jehovah, then, was not the only god. He was the only god of the Hebrews; but he was also "a great King of all the gods." These "all the gods" lived: only Jehovah was the great king over them, mightier than they, subduing them to his power, just as David subdued the petty kings that were his neighbors.

The next step beyond henotheism was monotheism,— the belief not only that men should exclusively worship one god, but that there was no other god to worship. This was one of the grandest steps that the religious life of man has ever taken; a step out of darkness into light. It was the dawn of the religious life of the world. How did man ever come to make such a stride as that? I propose to suggest just in a word — for I have time for nothing more — two or three reasons which would naturally lead men out of henotheism and into monotheism, out of the belief in many gods into the belief in one. 1. In the first place, the simple fact that the people exclusively worshipped one god would naturally develop in them the faith that he was the only one there was. 2. In the second place, political considerations, political pride, political growth and greatness, would tend in this same direction. As a people became great, and their god grew with their greatness, they would very naturally look down with scorn and contempt upon the gods of other peoples, and would naturally come to believe at last that they were no gods at all who could not defend their people and make them great or mighty. 3. And another thing, in the third place. I believe that one grand reason why the Hebrews came to be the first monotheists of which we have any knowledge was the absolute and fierce Mosaic prohibition of idolatry. You remember how astonished the Roman soldiers were, when they came to the temple of Jerusalem after they had battered down all opposition. They entered the holy place, and then pulled aside the veil and looked into the holy of holies. They stood in dumb amazement, for it was empty. They were hunting for the god of the Jews; and, when they came to the place where they supposed he made his abode, there was nothing there. And this was the one great reason, I believe, that operated more mightily than any other in developing the monotheism of the Jews. They worshipped an invisible, spiritual, and mighty power that pervaded all the earth. They came to worship such in their later life; and it was easy for them to draw a contrast and say, "Our god is alive, your gods are nothing but idols." And they flung at them their witty sarcasm and contempt, as in the lesson that I read you from the later Isaiah this morning. (Isa. xliv.) 4. Then of course there was working, in the fourth place, a growing sense of the law and order of the world. This is illustrated well in the story of Abraham, told by the rabbis. Of course, it has its origin many and many a hundred year this side the time of Abraham. It was said that at first Abraham was a sun-worshipper. No doubt he was. And he said as he looked at the sun, "This is my god, and I will worship him." But by and by night came, and the sun went down. And Abraham said, "That cannot be God who sets and is swallowed up by the darkness." Then the moon arose, and he said, "This is God, and these stars are the hosts of his followers." But by and by the moon set, and the stars, too, became dark; and he said: "These cannot be gods. The sun and the moon move in their regular round: they are under some law. I will worship him alone who makes that law and who controls their movements." Under these influences there would naturally spring up a belief in monotheism.

But still there is another step to be taken. They worshipped one god among the Jews. Among the Samaritans, they believed in only one god; but they still believed that this god was located, that he was attached to a place. One day, some one came to Jesus, and said: "Where shall we worship God? The Samaritans say we should worship him on Gerazim; the Jews say that we should worship him in the temple on Mount Moriah. You, as the Messiah, can settle this question." Then came that great ringing word which was the death-knell of a localized deity, which set God free and made him an inhabitant of eternity: "Neither in this mountain nor yet at Jerusalem shall men worship the Father. God is " — not *a* spirit. That little letter *a* is a huge mistake. Jesus said, " *God is spirit;* and they that worship him must worship him in spirit and in truth." Now, then, the race in the person of Jesus had attained free, spiritual monotheism.

And the Church, in the words of its articles, has declared from that time to this, what few, only a few, so far as I know, really think and believe,— that God is a being "without body, parts, or passions." These are the words of the thirty-nine articles of the Church of England. And yet is it not true that the great majority of Christendom still think of God as a body, as outlined, as localized, as living in some particular place, as sitting in some particular seat of power? But we must not look in church articles, if we want to find what the people really believe. Look at their poetry, their traditions, their myths, their stories. Dante tells us better than church articles what was the creed of the Middle Ages. In Dante, we find God in his *Paradise,* withdrawn from sight indeed, in a cloud so brilliant that the eye of man could not look upon it; and yet to Dante's thinking, and the thinking of the Middle Ages, God, in some sort of shape, outline, and power was there in that cloud as he was nowhere else. Take *Paradise Lost* as the expression of the faith of the English race. God there is simply another Jupiter, sitting on a throne in heaven and hurling thunder-bolts, organizing an army to drive out rebellious angels. And these angels, although they could not be mortally wounded, were capable of being thrust through with spears, being shot with arrows, capable of hurling craggy mountains through the air, and tumbling each other underneath their ragged ruins. This is a common picture of God, as living somewhere, sitting somewhere, ruling somewhere, more than he is anywhere else. I am not to-day to enter into the discussion as to whether this is true or not true. I simply aim to set forth what is the popular belief.

It now remains for me, as carefully and as briefly as possible, to outline for you the main theories concerning God that have filled the thought and that occupy the attention of the modern world.

1. In the first place, there is the theory that I have just spoken of,— God an outlined, visible being, somewhere outside of the universe. He lived alone through a measureless eternity. By and by, he waked up, and concluded to make something else to exist outside himself. He created matter out of nothing. Then he used this rough substance with which to build worlds,—made them as a carpenter builds a house, as a shipwright constructs a ship and sets it out there upon the ocean with its wings and sails. So he made these universes, and flung the stars off into space and told them to follow such and such paths forever.

2. Secondly, there is the theory that I may properly call "scientific atheism," the theory that says we do not need any god at all. "Only give me matter and force," say these men, "and I will account for the universe." And if you say to them, But where do you get your matter and your force? their answer will be,— what I think you will find a pretty hard one to reply to,—"It is just as easy for us to assume

our matter and our force as it is for you to assume your God." This is the position of scientific atheism.

3. The third position is pantheism. What is that? It is the belief that God is coexistent and cosubstantial with the universe; that nature is God, and God is nature. And that is all there is of it. That is pantheism.

4. Another belief, for which I have no name, I shall connect with the somewhat famous book written by two prominent scientific men of England, under the title of *The Unseen Universe*. They teach that there is a spiritual and invisible universe occupying the same space with this visible and tangible one; that the tangible universe has come out of that spiritual one, and returns to it again; that God is the life and the light and the power of both, manifesting himself in the spiritual realm and then in the visible realm, and that one is the shadow of the other. This these men claim is perfectly consistent with all known results of science; and I, at any rate, am not wise enough to contradict them.

5. The fifth theory of which I wish to speak goes by the name of "Agnosticism," — a common name in this age, one that stands for principles very widely held. It is the belief of those men who say man's faculties are limited; there is no possibility of his knowing anything except natural phenomena. There may be a God, or there may not be one; but, at any rate, we neither know nor can know anything about it. The man who takes that ground is called an agnostic.

6. There is still one more; and that is the belief in the immanence of God in the universe, — that is, a belief that God is the life and soul of this universe, in some such sense as what we call our mind is the life and soul of the body; that God is intelligence, that God is love, that God is will; and that he lives in and manifests himself through this universe, which is his body and of which he is the soul.

I have thus, as briefly and clearly as I could, traced for you the origin and the development of man's belief concerning God. It will be my business, in the following sermons of this series, to take up, one after another, the great questions that spring out of this theme, and try, if I can, to find out what we ought to think, what we ought to feel, what we ought to do.

DOES GOD EXIST?

I AM now to undertake the discussion of a theme than which there is none conceivable more profound or difficult. It is surrounded by so many misconceptions, so many misunderstandings, prejudices, hopes, and fears, that I hardly dare expect that I shall be in all cases understood, or make my discussion satisfactory to any large number of you. I shall leave one side almost entirely the old methods and the old arguments, and shall approach the theme in what, so far as I know, is a way new to sermonizing. I wish that you would bear clearly in mind the one single purpose that I have in view. I am not to raise the question as to whether a particular kind of god exists; whether there is a god in the universe answering to your mental picture or mine; whether there is a personal god or a conscious god; or, what are the characteristics and attributes of his being. These are themes that I shall hope to reach by and by. But they are beyond the possibility of this morning's discussion. I ask you then to keep in mind this one question, and this alone: Does there exist a being that we may properly call God? That and that only is my morning's theme.

A child new-born, and for long after its birth, is, so far as we know, unconscious of the distinction between itself and the things that are about it. The first step, then, that man takes in his knowledge of this wonderful world, is the discovery that there are at least two beings in existence, — himself and something outside that is not self. The next step that we take is the discovery that this not-self is the wonderful world, presenting itself to us under thousands of different aspects and forms and colors and forces. Here is, outside of ourselves, that exists independently of our volition, a being that as yet man has only begun to study and does not at all comprehend. This being,— call it world or universe or whatever you please, that presents itself to us under the shape of earth, grass, trees, brooks, rivers, mountains, clouds, oceans, and then the illimitable of stars and worlds all about us,— this being existed before we were born. It will exist after we have died. It lives then independently of us, and with no reference whatever to our volition. In some mysterious way, we trace this being as the source of our existence. Out of this being we have come; our bodies,— notice the significance of this,— our bodies not only, but our minds. Out of this mysterious fountain has come what we call "life,"— life in all its infinite range, whose thought sweeps from the abyss beneath our feet to the highest heavens over our heads, toward which we aspire. Out of it has blossomed foot and hand and brain; and out of this brain, thought and feeling, and love and hate, and hope and fear; not only an animal that hungers, but a Shakespeare who thinks, who dreams a Hamlet, a Goethe who dreams a Faust, a Jesus who dreams "Our Father in heaven," and bows down upon his knees in worship, and lifts up and thrills the hearts of the centuries by his words of religious inspiration and life. In some way, I say, all this has come out of this being, call it world or universe or what you will. "It," in the words of the old psalmist, "is *He*,"— shall I say it? Not yet. Suppose we substitute in place of He the word "it,"— for we do not propose to assume any thing,— and see if the wonder is lessened any: "It is" *it* "that hath made us, and not we ourselves." So much at any rate is scientifically true; and, if you can think it is any less wonderful that an *it* should make us than that a *he* should be our father, take the *it*, if you will. I am satisfied.

On this being, moreover, we depend every moment of our lives for all that we have of love and goodness, and happiness and peace, and beauty and hope. This being it is that, by and by, in spite of all our precaution, whether with or against our will, will call us away; and we shall cease to walk here among our fellows; shall be gone — where? This being, moreover, it or he, is our law-giver. In his laws or in its laws is life. It is by finding out the laws of this universe, and obeying them, that all the good of life comes to us,— all its health, all its genius, all its beauty, all its joy. May we not again, borrowing the words of the Psalmist,— for these parallelisms are wondrous and striking,— may we not again say, "In his" or its "favor is life"; and at its "right hand" — using a poetic figure — "there are pleasures for evermore"? For all the good, all the beauty, all the power of the world, come to us simply from knowing and obeying the will or the laws of this being. On the other hand, this is a being that inexorably, inevitably, and forever punishes the slightest infraction of its laws. In its favor is life, in its anger — to use a poetic figure again — is death. Disobedience to the laws of this being means diminution of life; carried far enough, means life's extinction.

This being again, how old is it? It is eternal. "From everlasting to everlasting, thou art"— not God,— I will not say that yet,— but "thou art." We will stop there. This being is eternal. We cannot possibly conceive a beginning, we cannot possibly conceive an end. Suppose we try to imagine a time when the sun and the moon and all this visible universe were not, when space was a blank. We can perhaps imagine such a time, but we cannot imagine a conscious living being existing for eternity in a blank; for it is a part of our very conception of life that it should act. Life means motion. And we must either conceive that things have existed forever, or we must conceive the absurdity of supposing that suddenly, without cause, something began to be.

This being, then, that surrounds us on every hand, is an eternal being. Not only that, it is an infinite being. As we cannot conceive a beginning nor an end, so neither can we conceive a limit anywhere. Suppose we take one little simple calculation, and use it as the lower step of a stairway by which I must leave your imaginations to climb toward a conception of the vastness of this universe. If a train of cars should start to-day and travel toward the sun at the rate of sixty miles an hour, and twenty-four hours a day, and three hundred and sixty-five days in a year, it would take more than one hundred and seventy years to reach the sun. And the sun is our next-door neighbor; and our solar system is a little flake of light on the borders of infinity. Think again. Light covers this distance between the sun and the earth, that would take a train of cars one hundred and seventy years to traverse,—light leaps that distance in a little more than eight minutes. And yet, travelling at that inconceivable speed, we know that there are suns so far away that it has taken thousands, millions of years for their light to reach us. May we not, then, say that this being is infinite? The scientific man, who sits with his pencil over his figures, knows that this is an infinite universe. Take the wings of this light, if you will, and travel to that star that the telescope has just caught a glimpse of, the light of which has been twenty-five millions of years in reaching the earth; and, when you are there, what? Only the first step out into this wilderness of worlds,— suns and stars and worlds still beyond. And suppose you could conceive of yourself as standing on the edge of the visible universe, and looking down into the very blank of space, what then? Space still, on and on forever. Or conceive a wall from the height of the zenith to the depth of the abyss,— space forever beyond your walls, no conceivable limit anywhere. This, then, is the infinite being that we are contemplating.

Not only infinite, it is also omnipotent. We talk of power. As in the case of distance, let me give you one or two simple figures to help your imagination to climb to a conception of some of the smaller manifestations of power. I hold a drop of water in my hand. Do you know how much power there is in that? The chemical force of that little drop of water is equal to that which is manifested by a flash of lightning that streams across the sky and the reverberating thunder that rings round the heavens. Do you know what the power of gravitation means? Do you know that, if you should take a bar of solid steel a mile square, and lay it beside the Catskill range of mountains, it would dwarf them, and their summits would be below its highest level? If you could attach such a mile-square beam of solid steel to the moon, do you think that would represent the power of gravity that holds the little orb of night in its place, as it circles about the earth? Think what the power of gravitation means, when I tell you that it would take eighty-seven thousand bars of steel a mile square to represent the power by which the earth holds the moon in its place! If you should cover the earth with threads of steel a quarter of an inch in diameter stretched from the earth to the moon, to hold the moon in its place, it would take enough of them to cover that side of the earth which is turned toward the moon with these steel spires only six inches apart. And this moon is only a little fragment, a worn-out asteroid; and our solar system is nothing in the deeps of space. Does omnipotence mean something to you in the presence of figures like that? We stand, then, face to face with an omnipotent being.

And then, again, this being that used to be worshipped under the phases of polytheism in its ten thousand forms, this being is now known to be essentially one, not many. The grandest result of modern science is the demonstration of the unity of the universe. That is what universe means. That is the significance that we find in the little word "cosmos": one, a system all bound together by unity,—unity of life, unity of law, unity of power. We are settling it rapidly—I think, beyond question—that all this material universe is one substance. The spectroscope has revealed to us the fact that in sun and moon and most distant star or flake of light on the farthest verge of the visible sky,—that all these contain in themselves the same metals and substances that constitute the globe on which we live.—Unity of substance throughout the universe. Chemistry has already reduced its elements to a very few; and the most far-sighted students of the world tell us that they expect by and by to find not fifty or sixty chemical elements, but only one; and that all the infinite diversity and variety of the world depend upon the multiplex arrangement and combinations of these simple elements.

And then we know, as beyond question, that there is only one power in the universe. One of the grandest results of modern science is the demonstration of what is called the "conservation and correlation of forces," or the "persistence of force." That is, there is only one force in the universe; and all the ten thousand varieties are manifestations, under different circumstances, of this one. For example, to illustrate in little what I mean, suppose I had suspended from the ceiling here to-day a rod of iron an inch in diameter. There is the substance which you see. Suppose I begin, by some machinery that enables me to move it very rapidly, to vibrate this bar of iron: there is motion. I move it more rapidly still, and soon your ear detects a sound, a buzz: this motion has become sound. More rapidly still, and it begins to glow, to become red-hot: motion has become color. More rapidly still, and it is white-hot, glowing with a light like the sun; and motion has become light. This simply as illustrating how all the different varieties of force in the world have been and are being translated one into the other. So we know that at bottom there is unity under it all.

This being, then, that surrounds us, out of which we have come, this infinite and eternal and omnipotent, is one being; as Tennyson phrases it,—

"One ——, one law, one element."

Shall we go on and repeat his next line?—

"And one far-off divine event,
To which the whole creation moves."

We may at least say this as the result of absolute demonstration: that there can be traced in the history of the universe, from the beginning until now, the progress of an intelligible purpose. I do not assume to say that the intelligence expressed in this is like our human intelligence. All I care for is simply this,— that here is a purpose running through the ages, linking them all together, that is intelligible to us. And this is intelligent in the only sense of that word which can have any meaning for us.

How far, then, have we got in the discussion of this theme? We have reached the point, I think, where I am justified in saying that we have a certain knowledge of a being who possesses all the attributes that are essential to

our conception of what we have been accustomed to call
God; a being self-existent; a being eternal, infinite, out of
whose life we have come; a being controlling us by its laws;
a being omnipotent; a being that is one; a being whose track
through the ages betrays the pathway of an intelligent purpose. Is not this what we have been accustomed always
to mean, when we have said "God"? Personality, as it is
ordinarily defined, is no necessary attribute of God. Personality, as we know it, carries with it limitation and mor-
tality. It is not necessary, then, to the completeness of our
conception of God, that we should say, in the ordinary use
of that word, that he is personal. It is not necessary that
we should say, in the ordinary use of that word, that he is
conscious. But what name can we give to a being who is
infinite and eternal and omnipotent, who creates life and de-
stroys, out of whom come intelligence, personality, thought,
will, love, hope, fear, aspiration, worship,— what word, I say,
will you use to symbolize a being like that? Not only this.
This one point more I must impress upon your attention.
This being, in some of its manifestations, has always inspired
in the human heart the sentiments of awe, of reverence, and
of worship: in grotesque and hideous forms, in the days of
barbarism; and in the highest and purest inspirations on the
part of the noblest poets and dreamers and prophets of the
world. What does Byron mean when he stands facing
the Alps, and says,—

> "To me high mountains are a *feeling*"?

What does he mean when he says,—

> "There is a pleasure in the pathless woods,
> There is a rapture on the lonely shore,
> There is society, where none intrudes,
> By the deep sea, and music in its roar"?

What does Wordsworth mean when he speaks of

>   .. " A presence that disturbs
> Me with the joy of elevated thought " ?

What does Bryant mean when, pausing before his ancient wood, he says,—

> " Father, thy hand
> Hath reared these venerable columns, thou
> Didst weave this verdant roof " ?

I only ask you to take these things as the natural poetic expression of human sentiment, nothing more. Only, is it not a little strange, is it not worth our while to stop just a moment and think of its significance, that one pile of dead, inert matter should make another body of dead, inert matter feel the sense of the sublime, feel like getting down on its knees to worship it? What is there in a pile of dead matter to worship? How has it come about that this sentiment of reverence and aspiration is called out by all that we name grand and magnificent in nature? These sentiments, friends, are facts, as solid facts as the ribs of the Rocky Mountains, as solid facts as the bones and fossils in your museums; and they demand an explanation as much as these. How does it happen, then, I say, that one particle of matter should want to get down on its knees to another particle of matter, if in both cases they are only dead and inert substance? And the absurdity is even heightened, if there is nothing but deadness and inertness in the universe around me, and I, a man, not dead and inert, have somehow come to feel a desire to bow and reverence and worship. It is utterly inexplicable. Search as you will, you will find no sensible explanation of it.

Now, then, shall we call this being God, or shall we call it Nature, or shall we call it Law, or Power, or Universe? Let me give you one reason that to me is conclusive why I must call it God. I shall not dictate as to the name which you shall apply. The word "nature," the word "universe," the words "law," "force," "power,"—all these have come to have attached to them a definite, dictionary meaning; and the meaning of those words excludes the idea of what we call conscious life. Now, then, I say, if you apply these words and these alone to the universe, you are doing an utterly unwarrantable thing; that is, you are assuming a settlement of this grand question, and assuming it in the negative. You are assuming that there is nothing but what you call matter here; when that is just the question that is filling the heart and thought of the world.

Suppose, for example, that in addressing you I should stop calling you man, and call you body. Body, in the use we have been accustomed to give to it, means the body when the life has gone. We speak of the body of the dead. We mean the body when that which we call mind and affection and thought have departed, no matter what they were or where they have gone. Body means death. But, when I call you man, I leave the question open. I do not say that you have a soul separable from your body, that can be taken out of it and exist somewhere else. I simply use a term that covers the body, and, if you have a mind and a soul, covers them too, leaving the question open. And so, when I use for this universe the word God, I do not use a word to express the idea that there is a god located in some place, or that there is a god separable from the universe who can go outside of it and look at it, as a man can go out and gaze upon his house. I simply use a term that covers the material universe, and, if there be anything more than what I call nature, covers that too. There is no other word then, so far as I know, in the range of human language, that we have a right to apply to this great being, except the name God.

Now, I want to raise the question — and answer it, if I can — as to whether this being about whom or which I have been speaking is matter, in the ordinary use of that word, or whether it is spirit. That is the great question on which the whole discussion turns. Is it not important enough, then, so that I have a right to ask you to think a little closely, if need be, to understand what I mean?

Suppose we call it matter. You may call it that, if you will: I will not quarrel about words; but, if you do, remember this, — you must change, even to utter reversal, your whole definition of matter. Call it matter, if you will; and yet, on that theory, you must admit that matter is something that thinks, matter is something that feels, matter is something that loves, matter is something that hates, matter is something that aspires, matter is something that worships other matter. If you call it matter, you must admit that definition.

Let us take our next step. We are accustomed to assume that matter is a very simple thing, to think we know all about it, and that the great mystery of the universe is mind. Matter, we say, — why, it is the every-day drudge: we stamp it under our feet; the wind blows it into our faces; we mould it into bricks, and of it build the walls of our houses. It is the brute beast that we ride and beat at our will. Why, we know all about matter. Mind, you think, is the thing that is mysterious. Matter is simple enough! And yet let me tell you, and ask you to think carefully until you see what it means, the only thing in this world about which we have direct, actual knowledge is mind. Even the existence of matter is an inference, and no subject of direct knowledge at all. It is mind of which we have direct and actual knowledge in our consciousness. And what do we know of the universe, of its suns and stars and systems and the various forms and forces of this world of ours? We only know and can study its images and reflections as they glass themselves in our consciousness. Let me illustrate what I mean: I put out my hand and touch this reading-desk. I say, There is something that is hard. What do I mean? I mean nothing more nor less than this: that there is a force there which thrills through the nerve of sensation in my arm, up into my brain, and translates itself into my consciousness as something that resists my touch. What this thing is that resists, nobody on the face of the wide earth knows. Take another illustration in regard to color. Suppose I had in my hand a book, the cover of which was blue. What do I mean by saying that it is blue? I mean simply that in a certain state of the light there is a sensation communicated to my optic nerve, which, running up into my brain, translates itself into my consciousness again as something which I call color. If it were night, and the gas were lighted, this same blue would be green. There is no blueness or greenness inhering in the thing itself: it is simply a sensation of mine, a phase of my own consciousness. This morning, when the organ was being played, I heard something that I called music. What do I mean by that, again? I mean simply that certain pulsations in the air are started by the touch of the organist upon the instrument, that those sensations communicate with my auditory nerve that runs into the brain, and that here those sensations are translated again into what I call consciousness. All I know, then, of this outside world, are facts of consciousness which are utterly unlike the outside world. So that all I can do is to infer certain things. All I know is that there is something outside of me,— a being, a power, a force, which manifests itself to me in these ten thousand different ways.

You know what a piece of matter is, do you? Let us look for it a moment; let us hunt, and see if we can find it. Suppose I have here in my hands a block of steel a foot square. I can apply to it a certain degree of heat, and it will become molten and run like water, as I saw tons of it running in the great steel manufactories of Sheffield. Apply still more heat, and it goes off into the air as a vapor, visible still; more heat, and it has eluded my senses, and is floating nobody knows where. Take this same piece of steel again. Do its particles touch each other? Is it perfectly solid? No. Because, if I apply to it sufficient force, I can compress it into still smaller space than it now occupies. That means that the ultimate particles, if there are any, do not touch each other. It is a part of our definition of matter that it is a centre of force; a something solid, so that no two particles of it can occupy the same place at the same time. These particles of the steel cannot touch each other so as to make the block all solid, or else I could not compress them any nearer together. And yet they hold themselves in their present position in some way, as though they were linked by hooks and bands; so that it would take the power of a thousand giants to pull them apart.

Scientific men tell us that force cannot exist apart from matter. Let us see the dilemma we are placed in, then, concerning this simple matter about which we supposed we knew so much. Two particles of matter, I have said, cannot occupy the same space at the same time, provided they are solid and substantial. And we know that the particles in this piece of steel do not touch each other, because we can compress it into a smaller space. Still, they exert force upon each other. We are now, then, face to face with a dilemma. Scientific men try to understand how it is that the power of the sun comes across the great gulf that separates it from our planet, so as to affect this earth. And, assuming as they do that force cannot exist where there is no matter, they say that this space between the earth and the sun must be filled with a very highly attenuated matter, which they call ether, becoming the medium of communication. They say that the interstices in this block of steel must also be filled with the ether, so that the force can pass through this ether from one ultimate atom to another. And yet, friends, see the absurdity of the dilemma in which we are placed. If every point of space is filled with a point of substantial matter, then all space would be solid; and movement of any kind, on the part of anybody or anything, would be impossible. And, if all space is not solid, then force not only does, but it must, exist where there is no solid particle of matter. This one dilemma, if you think of it and understand what it means, is the absolute death of what is called materialism. Force does exist where there is no solid particle of matter. Then there is no need of supposing matter to exist in order to explain force; and we are face to face with this grand fact which was the outcome and result of Faraday's deepest study: and Faraday was the greatest chemist of his age. He said that, when we pursue these ultimate particles of matter and try to find an atom, we find some mysterious thing that we can only call "a point of force." Matter simple, then? Nobody in the world can find it out. Nobody knows where it is or what it is. Seek for it, and it eludes your grasp like the shadow of a spirit. It melts away until all this grand universe, as Shakespeare dreamed,—

> "The cloud-capped towers, the gorgeous palaces,
> The solemn temples, the great globe itself,
> Yea, all which it inherit," do "dissolve,
> And, like this insubstantial pageant faded,
> Leave not a rack behind."

Matter is not a simple thing, then. It is the deepest mystery of the world.

One more point. I cannot possibly explain the fact that I

think and feel, if I am a materialist. You cannot possibly explain it, if you are a materialist. Consider for a moment. A thought or a feeling is utterly unlike what we call matter. A thought has no extension. Love is not hard. Neither of these has any color. Hope has none of the qualities that I attribute to this desk or to the book that I hold in my hand. And I cannot possibly explain the fact that I think and feel, in terms of matter. This much is true: I know that, every time I think, that thought is accompanied by certain molecular movements in my brain; and that thought in this way wears out the brain as much as shovelling wears out the hand. When Shakespeare was thinking of King Lear, and writing that wondrous play, he was wearing out his brain and was undergoing a physical strain, as much as a dray-horse when it drags its load of pig-iron. So much is true on the materialistic side. And yet no one can bridge the gulf between thought and matter.

One more step. While I cannot explain thought and feeling in terms of matter, yet, on the other hand, the universe, this wondrous, solid thing of which you have been accustomed to think, can be explained in terms of mind. I know what thought is and what feeling is. I have direct cognizance of them. And I can understand how it may be, and must be, that the universe should seem to me to be dead, although at the same time it may be alive. All I can be conscious of is the aggregate of feelings that makes up my personal consciousness. So this universe may be all thrilling and throbbing with a conscious life for aught I know; but it must seem to be unconscious and dead to me, because it does not come within the range of my consciousness. This, then, is all I wish you to understand on that point: that, while we cannot explain thought and feeling, if there is nothing but matter in the universe, we can explain this subtle, mysterious something that we call matter, on the supposition that there is nothing but that which we call spirit in the universe. This is no personal whim of mine, strange and startling as it may seem to you. The men that the pulpit fulminates against as materialists,— as Huxley, Tyndall, Herbert Spencer, and John Fiske,— all these great leaders of the modern thought of the world will tell you precisely the same truth. They are the great champions of anti-materialism, declaring it to be crude science and absurd philosophy. Mr. Huxley himself goes so far as to say deliberately that, if he must choose between the materialism of a man like Büchner and the idealism of a man like Berkeley, the facts of science compel him to be an idealist.

As the outcome of it all, then, what do we know,— not what do we guess, but how much do we know? I know, first, that life is, for I live. I know that thought is, for I think. I know that feeling is, for I feel. I know that love is, for I love. I know that hope is, for I hope. I know that aspiration is, for I aspire. I know that worship is, for I worship. These things we know; and such as these are the only things that, by direct consciousness, we do know. One more thing we know: while I do not know what matter is in itself, I do know that outside of, beneath, above, around me,— eternal, infinite, omnipotent, one,— I know there exists a life and a power back of phenomena, underneath phenomena, that manifests itself in these ten thousand different ways. Mr. Herbert Spencer will tell you that this, next to our own personal consciousness, is the one thing more absolutely certain than anything else in the world. We know that such a power as this exists. On the theory that this power is dead and inert matter, it is utterly inexplicable that I live. But, while I know that I live, it is perfectly explicable and rational that I should suppose that this being should also live, and at the same time seem to me, as related to my consciousness, the thing that I call matter. The one thing certain is that I live, the next thing certain is that this being exists. And the most rational explanation of it and of me is that this Being that exists is Life, with all that word implies and contains. So that I am justified, in the light of the most rigid demonstration, to close this morning by chanting the beginning of that beautiful hymn: —

> " Thou art, O God, the life and light
> Of all this wondrous world we see.
> Its glow by day, its smile by night,
> Are but reflections caught from thee.
> Where'er we turn, thy glories shine,
> And all things fair and bright are thine."

Agnosticism; or, Can We Know God?

AGNOSTICISM,— just what does the word mean, and what class of thinkers does it cover? As a school of philosophy, this agnostic type of thought has been more largely developed in Europe, on the Continent and in England, than it has here; though it is lying, in some loose way, in the minds of thousands of Americans, or floating cloud-like, though not clearly outlined, in all the theological air of the day. Agnosticism,— what is it? It is simply despair of knowledge in regard to the mysteries of the universe; it is giving up these great questions that have lured on the race from the beginning until now; it is saying: "It is of no use. These problems are insoluble. They are beyond the reach of the human intellect. There may be a god or there may not; but the world has never settled the question, and we see no prospect that it ever will settle it; so let us turn to something else." This, in brief and in general terms, is the type of thought that is covered by this word.

Now, however firm may be our faith, however irreligious to us or to any of us may seem a type of thought like this, one thing we must remember and look fairly in the face; and that is that whatever belief or unbelief is held by large numbers of thoughtful, earnest, scholarly men, is something not lightly to be brushed aside by a wave of the hand. And when we find men holding this position of agnosticism, who are as gentle, as true, as pure, as loyal to principle, as noble in their endeavor as are the most earnest and simple-hearted of religionists, we must admit that, whatever this is, it is something consistent with being good, grand, noble men. There must be a cause for this type of thought. Let us for a moment, then, at the outset, glance at two or three things that have conduced to bring it about.

It seems to me that it is perfectly natural, whether we find it justifiable or not. In the first place, it is a reaction, and a very justifiable reaction, against the old-time and very common assumption of an over-familiarity with God. Take up any one of the works of the old theologians, and you find that they talked as if they knew everything about God; as though it were not only an "open secret," but no secret at all. They understand God better than they know their next-door neighbors. They know what he was doing in the eternity before the world was created. They will tell you how the three persons of the Trinity formed a little select society by themselves, enjoying each other's company, carrying on conversations with each other; how they determined once on a time — why just then, no one knows — that they would create the world; how they settled it that that world should be created in such a way that this being, man, should certainly fall and become a rebel against God. And then, in order to bring about a deliverance from this evil which the gods or God himself had created, these three personalities entered into a covenant, which they call the "covenant of redemption," by which the Son agrees to be sent to suffer and to die, the Father agrees to send him and superintend his work, and the Holy Spirit agrees to undertake the completion and carrying out of that work after the crucifixion is accomplished. They tell us all about these things as though they knew God as intimately as they understood the management of their own town-meeting affairs. Is it not perfectly natural, as men developed in thought, as they developed in reverence even, in the finest qualities of the religious life, that there should be an earnest revolt against such assumptions of impious familiarity with the Infinite?

Not only did they revolt against this assumption of over-knowledge, but this doctrine of agnosticism has at its heart a moral quality. It is also a revolt against the unjust and immoral conception of God which has obtained in the ages of the past. They say: "If this be your God, we will have none of him. We will rather worship nature; we will worship humanity; we will do the best we can in the darkness; but we cannot bend our knees to a God whose character we cannot respect and whose attributes we cannot adore."

Then, the development of modern knowledge, the unveiling of this wondrous universe of ours, has conduced to bring about this type of thought. It was very easy to picture God in the old little universe,— the universe of Dante, the universe of Milton, the universe of the Old Testament,— a universe not nearly so large as our present solar system, which solar system we know to be an infinitesimal grain of sand on the seashore of infinity. It was very easy, I say, to conceive that you could know all about God, the god of a little world like that. But this universe has dissolved, — dissolved like a morning mist; and, as with opened eyes we look up and down and away, we see everywhere about us limitless infinity. And it seems to a thoughtful man the most unspeakable presumption that he should claim to fathom the unfathomable; that he should claim to know that which thought becomes weary even with trying to conceive. And I verily believe that the agnostic is more reverential in the truest sense of the word, is more religious, when he simply stands bowed in the presence of the unknown and the infinite, and says, "All this is beyond me,"— more reverential, more religious, I say, than the man who, with his little chart and compass and measuring-rod, is laying out, as he would an insignificant township, the limitless field of the absolute and eternal.

Then, as the world has progressed and modern knowledge has deepened, the old arguments concerning God have faded away. Take, for example, as an illustration of what I mean, the argument from design. That was the great weapon, you remember, of men like Paley. Paley's watch has become very famous in theological discussion. He said, I trace everywhere in this watch evidences of design; and design indicates a designer. So of the manifest adaptations in nature. A flower, for example, is adapted to the place where it grows. One kind of flower is adapted for life in the tropics: it grows in the tropics. Another is adapted to live close up by the snow-line, on the highest peaks of the Alps or the Andes; and another is adapted to live somewhere else. Or, for example, on some islands of the Pacific, you find that the insects are almost wingless, unable to sustain themselves for any time in the air. All these, and the thousands like them, betray a designing mind. But the scientist explains all these facts by saying: Of course, you see this which seems to you like design; but it is all easily accounted for by the law of natural selection. A flower grows in the tropics, you say. Why? It is adapted to live in the tropics, therefore it was designed to live there. No, says the scientist: it lives in the tropics just because it is the product of, and so adapted to, its surroundings; and, if it were not adapted to its surroundings, it would die. Therefore, that which lives is adapted to its surroundings, and must be. So, in regard to these wingless insects of the Pacific islands.

Why are they wingless? What is the secret of this curious adaptation? These islands, being largely bare of vegetation, are swept by the winds from one year's end to the other; and those insects which possess wings and lift themselves up into the air are blown off into the sea, and perish. Only those that are wingless, and keep thus close to the ground, survive and propagate their kind. Of course, they are adapted to the place! If they were not, they would die out. Thus, they tell us they can dispense with the old argument from design. I believe that, so far as I have carried it this morning, they are right. This, however, does not preclude that which I spoke of last Sunday as an indication of an eternal, ever-unfolding purpose running through the ages. By purpose, I only mean that which to us looks like purpose, and corresponds to our intelligence.

Another reason why they tell us we cannot know anything about God is based on what, so far as I know, is now universally accepted as a fundamental principle in modern science; that is, the "relativity of knowledge." What do I mean by that? Simply this,— that we have found out that we cannot know anything except as it is related to us. I do not know what this book is "in itself." I touch it, and it feels hard. I look at it, and it appears square and of a brownish color. I strike it on the desk, and I hear a sound. If I should taste it, I should find a flavor in the paper or ink or leather of which it is made. It manifests itself to me through all these different senses. But what it is beyond that, or whether it is anything beyond that, I do not know. My knowledge of it is purely relative, relative to my faculties of perception. And so they say that here is a limit beyond which no man can pass. Thus, we can never know what this great Being about which we are speaking is in itself or himself. We can only know phenomena, manifestations of life, as they are related to our faculties of perception. Therefore, they say,— and the conclusion seems to be very rational and logical,— since we can never know anything of this infinite and eternal essence, if such there be, let us confine ourselves to the possible and the practical. I agree with them. Let us confine ourselves to that which is possible and practical. But will some one please to tell me what is possible and what may be practical in its application to our human life? That man, that nation, which has ever done anything in the world from the beginning until now, has been the one that has earnestly believed in the possibility of the impossible. No nation ever was great, no man ever was great, who had the word "impossible" in his dictionary. Is there anything impossible? You may tell the navigator, the student, the scientific man of the world, as long as you will, that they can never reach the north pole, and that, if they could, it would do no good. But men have always been knocking at the icy door of the Arctic, and they are knocking there to-day. And, in spite of all your wise advice, they will knock there until it opens. A north-west passage or a north-east passage, or a passage over the ice fields, will be found. For it is the most glorious quality of this human nature of ours that it will not admit that any door cannot be opened. It believes with all its heart that which Jesus has said, "Knock, and it shall be opened." It has knocked, and it will knock, and it will knock forever. Impossible! Why, a thousand things that were once impossible are of every-day occurrence now. It was once impossible to build a ship to sail over the seas; but it was done. It was impossible that this little puffing breath of steam should enable men to control their ships so as to sail right in the teeth of the wind and the tide, and defy the storms,— impossible to do this; but it was done. It was impossible to construct railroads so that they should bridge the rivers and tunnel the mountains and reach from one end of the earth to the other,— impossible, all men said, except a few dreamers; but it was done. And what is there that is impractical? What is there that is of no use for man to know? No one has knowledge profound enough to say of anything, There is no use in studying that. There have been those who would take astronomy from the schools and confine our attention simply to this world. But the stars themselves are the guides of men in sailing the oceans of the world. These far-off and once inaccessible powers and forces of the universe are to-day the common ministers to the wants of man. What was the use of Franklin's going out with his kite, and trying to see if he could tease the lightning to come down out of the cloud and perch upon his hand? Suppose he could, what of it? A mere piece of curiosity! And yet has not the result of that purely speculative scientific curiosity changed the face of the world, and given us a new type of civilization? And this marvellous power that flashed and leaped with its terrible joy, from storm-cloud to storm-cloud, has become an every-day servant, a common minister to the every-day man of the world.

There is nothing that the world will believe to be impossible. There is nothing that the world will believe may not be turned to practical account. And I, for one, am not ready to admit that a knowledge of God, if it can be found, is of no practical value to the world. You know well enough that I do not believe that a knowledge of God would change the standards of our daily living. I believe the principles of morality have been developed by the social life and experience of man; and, whether there is a God or is not, truth and right, and purity and justice, and goodness, and all these moral qualities of the world, remain the same. And yet a belief in God, even in the sphere of morals, would be the most intensely practical thing of which the world could conceive. I will do the best I can, if I know I shall die to-morrow. I will do justice; I will try to help those that are needy; I will do all I can to make the world happy and good, whether I am to live in the future or not, whether there is a God in the heaven that will care or not. But suppose I know that there is intelligence and love in the deeps of the infinite above me; that I am the child of God, and that he cares what I do, whether I do or do not these things that I know are right; that he watches the burdens that I carry; that he knows the sighs and sufferings of my heart, the temptations that beset me; that he understands the struggle through which I pass,— no matter whether he touches my burden by the lightest weight of a finger; no matter whether he clears off the cloud that makes it dark before my way; no matter whether he does anything except sit there silent,— if I know the intelligence and the love are there, it becomes the mightiest mainspring and motive of life of which it is possible to conceive. It does not change our standards; but it does put a deeper meaning, an infinite meaning, into life. I believe then that the world will try to find out about God. You may prove to them just as often as you please that it is useless, and that, if it were not useless, it would be utterly impossible: still, the world will never give up the quest. Let us then turn and look it in the face for a little while.

In the first place, let us raise the question as to what instruments of research are in our hands. By what method shall we seek to find out God? Have we any faculties adequate to such an endless quest? I believe that there is only one method of knowledge in the universe, whether the object of that knowledge be God or man or fossil, whether it be duty or the knowledge of a flower, whether it be in the heavens above or in the earth beneath or in the depths under the earth. There is only one possible method of knowledge and that is the method of science. What do we mean by science? Not merely a knowledge of animals, of trees, of mountains, of fossil bones, of stars,— not that alone which is called physical knowledge. Science is a method; and it applies to every possible phase of knowledge with equal propriety and force. It means observation, verification, comparison, putting the things we have observed and verified together. Then, if we can discover the links that bind our phenomena in one, we shall have a philosophy of science. I believe this is the only method by which we can seek and find God, or anything else in the universe.

Now let us glance over a few of the other methods that are proposed, and see if they do not come within the scope of this. For example, they tell us that miracles have occurred, and that these prove the existence of God and manifest the qualities of his character. If miracles have occurred, they are facts to be observed, to be proved, to be estimated as to their quality and value. So they come within the scope of the scientific method equally with anything else.

They tell us that God has given us a revelation of himself in a book. I for one cannot accept this statement as true. I remember a gentleman who, on a certain occasion, said he did not believe in ghosts, because he had "seen too many of them." I cannot believe in revelations, because I have seen too many of them. Which one shall we believe, the revelation of our religion or of some other man's religion? There are at least a half-dozen great books in the world that claim to be the direct gift of God. But suppose God has given us a book. Then this book is a fact, a reality, something to be observed, to be verified, to be estimated as to its quality and value. It comes then within the scope of the **scientific method.**

Again, they tell us that we must know God by faith. What do they mean? Faith is not credulity. It is not believing a thing without any evidence. If it is, it is unworthy of a rational man. Faith,— what is it? What do I mean when I say I have faith in a fellow-man? I mean that I know something of that man, his character, his career, his conduct in the past, his capacity, so that I believe in him as to what he will do in the future, what he is capable of achieving. I have faith in him. If faith means anything rational and worthy, it is based on the result of knowledge and experience in the past, and is simply an assertion as to what we believe will occur in a new set of circumstances similar to those with which we are already familiar. Suppose I say I have faith in God,— and, friends, I have, and I believe it is rational, I believe it is justifiable,— what do I mean? I believe that the experience of the past history of humanity has given us reason to have faith in to-morrow. I stand facing the unknown; and I say, I believe, I trust. And I walk forward into the cloud, though I cannot see the next step before my feet. If there is no past experience of humanity justifying a faith like this, then it is sheer madness, it is an impulse of insanity, and not of reason. Faith, then,— what is it? It is the result of the past experience of the world; it is facing the unknown, and trusting it on the basis of that past experience. The foundations, then, of this faith, are objects of knowledge, of observation, of experiment, of scientific verification and proof. So faith itself, then, comes within the scope and limits of this scientific method.

Men tell us about heart-knowledge,— I hear it perpetually in ministerial conferences and from the pulpit,— they tell us we must know God not through the head, but through the heart. What do they mean? I can find no meaning in it save this: that, if I am to know another being who lives or has feeling, I must come into contact with that being through sympathy. This heart-knowledge, this sympathy, then, is simply a sort of sixth sense, another perceptive power, a faculty by which I reach out and come into contact with some other being or power or life around me. I take Shakespeare in my hand, and I say, I cannot understand Shakespeare, except as I have the poetic quality in my nature that brings me into sympathy with him. True. This sympathy becomes a faculty by which I perceive the qualities of Shakespeare that I would not perceive, if I did not have the sympathy. And precisely the same thing is true of anything else. Take the case of one of my senses. If I had no sense of touch, I might have the sense of sight, taste, hearing, and smell, but I could come into relation with only a part of what I say makes up this book which I hold. I can only come into relation with those parts of it for which I have the proper perceptive faculties. I can know God then, I can know something of the grandeur of the world, only as there is in me a sympathy that reaches out and comes into contact with these facts and qualities of the world about me. But, when the heart has felt, that feeling is a fact: it is a fact to be observed just as much as the fossil itself. It is a fact to be intellectually estimated and weighed and assigned its place. So this heart-knowledge, this sympathy, comes also within the scope and limits of the scientific method.

Theodore Parker was the great theological representative in this country of what is called Transcendentalism, the intuitional method. But science has explained intuition. It is the result of human experience; and, in so far as a man's intuitions are justifiable, they are a part also of the scientific method.

Professor Max Müller, of London, tells us that he believes that man has a direct perception of the infinite. Granted. I believe he has. But this perception again is the perception of a reality. And so through whatever avenue of the mind I go out and come into contact with the world around me, when I have come into contact with it, I have found a reality, a fact, a something to be perceived, to be observed, to be verified, to be dwelt with intellectually according to its value. The scientific method, then, is the only method by which anything in the heavens above or the earth beneath can be known.

I come now to that which is the crucial part of my discussion, that to which the points I have been taking up thus far are only steps. With this scientific method in my hands now, can I really know God? That is the great question that I wish now suggestively and as briefly as possible to answer. You are more or less familiar with the doctrine, which has become famous in these modern days, of the "Unknowable." It is chiefly connected with the name of Herbert Spencer. He teaches that God is unknown, and must be forever unknown. But he does not teach it with any more emphasis than does the Bible. "Canst thou by searching find out God?" "It is high as heaven, what canst thou do? deeper than the abyss, what canst thou know?" "No man hath seen God at any time." He is the infinite, forever eluding us, always beyond. But, now, what precisely does Herbert Spencer mean by his doctrine of the Unknowable? We will see, then, whether it precludes the possibility of all knowledge. He says that knowledge is only a process of classification. Let me illustrate, following his suggestion, but not literally quoting him. Suppose I am walking out in a field. The wind does not blow, and the air is still; but, in spite of this fact, I see the tall grass moving at a distance. I say, There is something alive. I class that motion with other motions that indicate life; and I feel that some living thing is the cause of that motion. I walk on, and soon a dog springs up out of the grass and runs across the field. What do I mean when I call it a dog? I have not explained anything. I have merely classed that particular dog with all the other members of the species that go under that name. I get near enough to him, and I say, It is a Newfoundland dog. I have completed another process of classification. Not only a dog, but I have narrowed the range of my thought to a particular kind of dog. Then, as I get nearer to him, and make a closer examination, I know of what color he is, whether black or white or a mixture of the two. And so I may proceed as far as I please; but all the time I am only carrying on a process of classification. Herbert Spencer tells us that this is what we mean by knowledge. Why cannot we know God then? Why? For the simple reason that God is one, unique, unlike anything else in the universe,— the one, the infinite, the eternal. Of course there is no possibility of classifying Him, since there is no second with whom he can be compared. That is the famous doctrine of the Unknowable. With this definition of knowledge, are we not all compelled to accept the conclusion?

But now does that preclude the possibility of knowledge? Let us see if the same difficulty does not apply to any thing else in the world. Take the case of my nearest and dearest friend. I do not know what that friend is "in himself." I know first the clothes he is accustomed to wear, his external appearance; his look, the tone of his voice. I get acquainted by conversation with the type of his thought and the extent of his intelligence. I get familiar after long association with the kind of character that he bears. But all the time I simply know certain manifestations that he makes of himself to me. I do not know him completely, and I never can know him completely. I do not know what he is in essence. So I may take a flower, and precisely the same truth holds here. Take this rose that I hold in my hand. I do not know it completely, I cannot know it completely. I smell it, and know its fragrance. I touch it, and know the feeling of stem or leaf. I look at it, and know its color. But we know perfectly well that our senses do not exhaust the universe. We know there are millions and millions of air-waves that do not translate themselves to our ear as sound. We know there are other millions of other waves that do not transmit themselves to our eyes as light. And we have reason to believe that the universe is infinite above and beneath and beyond us on every hand, forever eluding us; for the simple reason that we have no adequate faculties to bring ourselves into contact with it all. If I could know this flower, if I could know it completely, I should know everything. You remember those famous words of Tennyson:—

> "Flower in the crannied wall,
> I pluck you out of the crannies;—
> Hold you here, root and all, in my hand,
> Little flower,— but if I could understand
> What you are, root and all, and all in all,
> I should know what God and man is."

The universe is all one piece. I catch hold of some loose thread of this infinite garment of God,— that is forever being woven, and is never done,— and it leads me face to face with the Infinite. It starts a question that no man can answer. Precisely this same quality of the Unknowable, then, attaches itself to the most commonplace thing of life. I can only know certain manifestations. I can know nothing in its essence. It is just as true of my book, or my coat, or my friend, or this flower, as it is of God.

There is another thing that they warn us against, that I

must speak of, in order to complete my thought. They tell us we must beware of that long word, anthropomorphism. What do they mean? It is that we are in perpetual danger of thinking of God as though he was like ourselves. That is, — to illustrate what I mean, — I have no right to say that God plans, without explaining that word. Why? Why, when a man plans something, it means that he thinks out a problem that he does not know as yet. He overcomes certain difficulties that are in his way. We cannot conceive of any problem that the Infinite does not know, so that he has to plan or think it out. There are no difficulties that the Infinite has to overcome. Of course, it is not proper for us, in that sense of the word, to speak of God as planning. We cannot speak of God as thinking, in the same sense in which we think; for all that we know about thinking is connected with certain processes and movements of the human brain. Unless God has a brain, he does not think as man thinks. And yet, if we are not anthropomorphic, if we do not speak in symbolical language, derived from human thought and human experience, we shall never be able to speak at all. We are just as anthropomorphic about other things as about God. We talk of the sky as frowning or smiling. We talk of the waves on the seashore as sobbing or the wind as sighing. We talk of the sun as rising and as setting. We talk about the universe, in every direction, in this symbolical language; and nobody says we must not use such speech about the daily facts of life. Nobody is in danger of being mistaken; for we know, in the natural world, that we are able only to symbolize the reality. I do not know how we can help being anthropomorphic concerning God. I am certainly nearer the truth when I say God thinks than when I say he does not think; although, when I say he thinks, I cannot mean that he thinks in the same way as I do. If I say God loves, I can hardly mean that he loves in the same sense, precisely, in which I love. And yet we must not think of God as something less than thought, less than purpose, less than love, but as something infinite, transcending all these modes of speech and life with which we are familiar. We must be anthropomorphic, then; and there is no harm in it, if we only remember that language, in every direction, is but a symbol, and an inadequate symbol at that; and that, when we put our thought into speech, we have only outlined shadows and reflections that are not adequate to express the reality.

Now, I am prepared to say, in the face of all that the modern world knows, and in spite of all the difficulties that we have been considering, that we may know God, and that we do know God, in precisely the same sense in which we may know and do know anything else whatsoever. I may know God just as I may know my friend. I may know him just as truly, just as really, and, I say again, in precisely the same way. The only difference is a difference of degree, not at all a difference in kind. I can know more of my friend because he is on my level; and the finite can never exhaust the infinite. Now, to say in a word just what I mean by this statement,— that may seem to many of you irrational and startling — all I know of any of you, of this flower, this desk, this table, this platform, all I know of these windows through which the light streams in, all I know of the sun, all I know of the earth beneath my feet, all I know of anything, is *certain manifestations* of these that come to me through my senses and perceptions. I do not know what they are in themselves, and never can know.

Now, the one thing, scientific men tell us, that we know more certainly than we know anything else outside the limits of our own consciousness, is the existence of this power and life back of and manifesting itself through the phenomena of the world. I know these manifestations; I study them, I compare them; I verify them; I classify them; and, instead of saying that we know nothing about God, I believe it is perfectly proper for us to say that *we know nothing else but God*. For everything in the universe is simply so for a manifestation of this infinite power and life that we call God.

Just one word more: we are in the midst of mystery, a mystery that we shall never be able completely to penetrate. This is something that grows out of the nature of things, a necessity, and — as I shall show you in just one moment — a blessing. Suppose I am standing on the deck of a ship in mid-Atlantic some foggy morning. Perhaps I cannot see more than ten feet away from me in any direction. I see dim shadows, outlines of a few things just in the edge of the mist. I have a very small realm, and I can know a good deal about it: I can know it quite completely, because it is small. But, as the sun rises, the fog lifts. The circle of the visible enlarges, until by and by the whole ship stands out clear against the sky, and the fog is lifted from all the sea. I can see clear to the horizon, miles on miles of waves lifting and sinking, and other ships passing to and fro from different ports of the earth. The world of the known and the visible is increased and widened. So also, and by this same process, the world of the unknown and the invisible is increased; until just as I know a great deal more and can see a great deal more than I did before, so there is a wider circle beyond which I cannot see and cannot know. Suppose I am standing in a valley, at the foot of a mountain. I can see only a little around me, and I can understand it very well. I begin to climb up the mountain-side. My horizon widens on every hand, and by the time I am on the summit the world is at my feet. I see more, but the wall of the unknown is also widened, and extends beyond me on every hand.

I take a glass, and sweep the skies above my head. Though my eyes travel for millions and millions of miles, there only grows on me the sense of worlds forever and forever beyond, eluding me at every advance, things which I can never know.

So we may study and travel for eternity, and the mystery of the universe will only deepen at every step; for everything we shall ever learn will only broaden the horizon of that which is beyond us. Is this thought oppressive? It is the only hope for man. If the universe were small, and my brain, my capacity of thought and investigation, were small, corresponding to the size of the little universe, I might study it and look it all through, and then — despair! The end reached, nothing more to think about, nothing more to live for! This would be the death of the world. If I could exhaust infinity, I should merely be reading my own death warrant. Immortality would be an absurdity, even as a thought, to a man who could read clear through the nature of things. But, just because we are finite, just because this is an infinite universe, we may take the wings of the morning and fly to the uttermost parts of the sea, we may leap from world to world through an infinity of space, and still infinity is beyond; new fields, grand careers, avenues unentered inviting us on every hand. Thus, it is rational to dream that we may study and think and live and love forever! And the universe, around us, beneath us, above us, grander and grander still and ever inviting us on, may still open before us infinities and eternities unattainable beyond.

Is God Conscious, Personal, and Good?

WE are, I trust, by this time convinced that God is, that he is eternal, infinite, almighty; that by the method of science,— the only adequate method of human research with which we are acquainted,— we may rationally investigate and hope to know something of his methods, his ways, his manifestations throughout the universe, and in the life, character, and history of man. But we want to know something more than this. The one great thing, it seems to me, for which our human hearts hunger, is to know, not whether we are dealing with omnipotence, infinity, eternity, but whether we are dealing with thought, with a heart. Is it an infinite and almighty and at the same time a deaf and blind and heartless giant with which, like Jacob in the darkness, we wrestle and struggle throughout the long night of our human career? If so, then we inevitably fight a losing battle. However successful it may seem to be for a time, however we may conquer these mighty, dead, blind forces, and for a while make them serve us, still, day by day, week by week, year by year, this mighty power is getting the better of us. We are growing older and weaker; our physical and mental powers are gradually waning and wasting; and, do what we will, the giant will throw us at the last: our feet will slip, and we shall fall into that dark and fathomless abyss that we call the grave. I say what we want to know is whether we must take this view of life,— for we must take it, if God be not conscious, as much as personal, and loving,— or may we feel that, though we are compelled, for reasons as yet at least partially inscrutable, to carry burdens that chafe our shoulders and crush our hearts, there is some one in the universe that cares? When our hearts sigh in the midst of their sorrow, may we believe that there is sympathy outside that notices that sigh? When our hearts ache, may we believe that there is somebody who notices that they ache, somebody who cares that they ache, somebody who would lift off the burden and assuage the pain, were there not some grander, deeper reason that urges silence and waiting until the result of the sorrow be achieved? This, then, is the question: Does God think, does God care, does God love; or are we dealing with forces mightier than we, that we are compelled to think of as heartless, and to which we may cry in vain as long as we will, because they are deaf and unconscious?

You will remember that, in the last sermon of this course, on Agnosticism, I dealt with the question of our being anthropomorphic; that is, of our being compelled to speak of God and of all things in the world in language drawn from human thought and human experience. That is, I said, if we speak of God as planning, we cannot mean that he plans in the same sense that we do,— recognizing difficulties, and devising means by which he may overcome them. This is a figurative way of speaking, drawn from human experience. I said we were anthropomorphic, whether we were speaking of God, or whether we were speaking of a flower or a grain of sand or a star. We cannot help being anthropomorphic, until we can escape the limitations of our nature. I shall speak, then, anthropomorphically to-day, claiming not only the right, but asserting the necessity of this use of language,— only asking you to remember what I called your attention to then, that we must not for one moment forget that all our language is, and of necessity must be, symbolic. It does not express the absolute, the complete, the final truth, when we speak of the infinite; for our language is finite. Our words are coined and minted in human experience and human observation. Finite words cannot be completely true, when we are dealing with these great themes. And yet remember this: although it may not be philosophically accurate for me to say God thinks, because thinking, with us, is connected with the human brain, for me to say God feels, for feeling, with us, is connected with a system of nerves; that God loves, for love is strictly a human experience, as we understand the word,— though it may not be scientifically correct for us to use these terms, yet they are the best terms, indeed, the only terms, we have; and we must either use these, or keep silent. We may remember, however, that, when we say God thinks, God feels, God loves, we are not overstating the reality, but infinitely undertating it. We are using a human shadow to express a divine reality, and we know that the reality infinitely transcends the shadow. With this explanation, then, I shall go on and fearlessly speak in these terms of human thought and human feeling, asking you to make due allowance wherever such terms occur.

Our first question, then, is as to whether God may be rightly thought of by us as a conscious being. It may seem strange to some of you that such a point as this should ever be raised. And yet it is one of the great philosophical questions of the world at the present time, over which the keenest intellects are striving. Hartmann, the prince of pessimists, that great German philosopher, the principle of whose system is that this is the worst possible kind of a universe that could be conceived,— Hartmann goes on at length and elaborately, by the use of scientific facts and arguments, to demonstrate that God is a being who thinks and who wills. But it is also the fundamental principle of his system that this great thinking and willing being is unconscious. So his philosophy goes by this name: it is "The Philosophy of the Unconscious." He believes that God thinks and wills, and that he has arranged all this universe, but has done it like a giant in a dream, absolutely unconscious all the time as to what he was about. But the point that I wish to call your attention to, and that which has led me to mention him at all, is this: that he has scientifically demonstrated that there is will and intellect manifest in the universe. I want to spend just a moment over these two points, and then let you see what bearing they have on the question of consciousness.

Is there any manifestation of will in the universe? There is, at any rate, what Matthew Arnold calls a "stream of tendency." The universe, from the first beginning of it that we can trace until now, has pursued a definite and intelligent line of movement, as though, at any rate, there was a will manifested in and propelling the entire course of universal progress. What do we mean when we speak of will as connected with a man? How do I know, for example, that any of you will to do a certain thing? If we have not thought a great deal about it, perhaps we are accustomed to suppose that there is some independent power in us that goes by the name of will, something that sits on a little throne, something that controls the movement of the hand, the foot, the thought. But, if you will only give it a little calm consideration for a moment, you will see that all we mean by it, all we possibly can mean, is that the man wills to do that which he does, wills to think that which he really thinks, and wills to accomplish that which he strives after. That is, the will is simply the resultant of all the forces that make up the being. If we stand by the bank of a river, we see it flowing in a certain direction, north or south. There are eddies, counter-currents and curves and turnings of the river, but on the whole it sweeps with its whole force in a certain direction. So we may observe concerning a man; may observe, as we think, concerning the operations of our own consciousness. There are eddies, there are counter-currents, there are conflicting interests and desires, but at last we will. What do we mean? We mean that the resultant of all these influences and forces is that we move in a certain direction. That is all we mean by will. It is all we can mean in an intelligent use of language. Now look over the universe, look over human history, look over all that we know concerning this wonderful world, and we see everywhere from first to last the sweep of tendency, this intelligible motion onward. And we have precisely the same right to assert of this the existence of will that we have to say that will exists in the heart or the brain of any one of our fellow-men. Will, then, or that which corresponds to it in man, is demonstrable as a fact, an eternal reality in the universe.

Does intelligence exist in the universe also? Again, what do we mean by intelligence, when we are speaking of its manifestation in men? I cannot get at the movements of my brain to know what intelligence may be in its essence, whether it is essentially connected with the brain or not; and, if I cannot reach it in my own case, much more I cannot reach it in any of you. What do I mean then, when I say that Mr. A. or Mr. B. is an intelligent man? I mean simply this: that his words and actions correspond to what I call the logical and rational order of my thought. That is all I mean, that is all I can mean. If they do not thus correspond, what do I say of him? I say he is odd, he is eccentric, he is irrational, perhaps insane or an idiot. What do I mean by these words again? I mean only that his words and his actions do not correspond to the logical and rational order of my thinking. All I know then of human intelligence outside of myself is just this,— the force of which I wish you to carefully note,— that the words and actions of people outside of me do correspond to the logical and rational order of my own thought. Now, then, I look abroad over the universe, over its past history and its present condition, and do I not see everywhere a most stupendous order, — from the chemical constituents, and their relations, that make up a drop of water; from the orderly arrangement of leaves upon the branch of a tree; from the marvellous and inflexible order and arrangement of the parts that make up a crystal; clear up to the sweep of stars and constellations over my head,— everywhere a stupendous, an infinite, a majestic order, a movement that corresponds, just so far as I can rise to the magnificent idea of it, to the logical and rational order of my thought? If, then, I have a right to say that man is intelligent, I have an infinitely grander right to say that there is intelligence, or that which transcends what we mean by that word, in the universe.

God, then, wills. God, then, is an intelligent being. And I have a perfect scientific, demonstrable right to use these words concerning God in the only sense that they have in the dictionary, in the only way in which they are properly used concerning our fellow-men. Now, then, if there be intelligence and will in the universe, have I not a right to say that this intelligence and this will are conscious? No man has ever yet known anything of the existence of will and intelligence as separated from consciousness. You may tell me, if you choose, that I walk unconsciously, that I perform half the actions of my life unconsciously, and that these actions betray intelligence. You may tell me, if you choose, of well-authenticated cases of men composing in their sleep, as did Coleridge, and making a beautiful poem unconsciously; or of another man's rising in his sleep, and working out some deep mathematical problem unconsciously. I grant it all; but all these cases are simply the result of habit. In the first instance, the work was conscious. In the first instance, the poetic composition was conscious. The work of applying mathematical principles was conscious work. They are unconscious simply as the result of habit. But, in the first instance, all the activities of man, all the activities of which we know anything,— intelligence and will,— are conscious activities. And, if we reason — as alone we have the right to reason — from the known to the unknown, wherever we find intelligence, wherever we find will, we are forced by the logic of our own reason, as far as our knowledge extends, to assert also that this will and this intelligence are conscious. For lack of time, then, to elaborate further, I leave my first point here. I believe, that carefully considered, these thoughts that I have urged are scientific demonstrations that God is a conscious being.

Now, then, is he personal? That which I have already been saying bears largely on the solution of this new problem. And yet there are certain things about it that I must take up and look at by themselves. In the first place, we must do what, if more frequently done, would make a good many questions clearer than they are: we must settle a definition. What do we mean when we talk about personality? Is it not true that what people really are anxious to know when they are discussing the question of the personality of God is that he thinks, that he loves, that he cares? That is what they mean, is it not?

Now, then, let us look at this word "personality" and see

what its significance is. Of course, God is not personal in the sense in which we use that word in our sitting-rooms and on the street every day. We say, There goes such a person along the street: what do we mean? Why, there is a being outlined, having a definite form and shape, occupying a specific locality in space; a being who, in his personality, is subject to all conceivable limitations; a being who is sick, who suffers, who hopes, who fears, who is pained, who is troubled; a being who by and by must die. All those elements go to make up the meaning of the word "personality" as used on the street. Certainly, we cannot think for a moment that we are to attribute these characteristics to God. God is not a person in the sense in which we are accustomed to use that word.

Now, where does this word "personal" come from? It is derived from an old Latin word, which originally stood for the mask of an actor. In the old Greek and Roman theatres, an actor always wore a mask, which represented the character he was to assume; and this mask was called *persona*, the personality that could be put on and taken off. Open Shakspere, and you will find at the head of the plays the words *Dramatis Personae*, persons of the drama. The word originated then here. It is the character or part which the actor assumes at a particular time or place, which first bore the name "person." But we do not mean that by it now; and, if we are to keep that old meaning, then we must think of God not as unipersonal or tripersonal, but multipersonal. For, whenever God manifests himself in any way or form, whatever mask he may assume in the heavens above or the earth beneath, this manifestation becomes a personality in the original meaning of the word.

But though we are not at liberty to say that God is personal, as we are accustomed to define the term, yet — mark this, for the whole discussion hinges on this one thought — we are not at liberty, in denying God's personality, either to say or to think that he is something less than personal. Suppose I close the shutter of my study window, and only let a little, tiny, white ray of light come through. Then, I take a prism in my hand, and I split up this ray into the various colored parts of which it is composed. I fix upon the red. Have I a right to say that the ray of light is red? No. It is white. And I assert that which is untrue, if I fix upon any one of its specific colors, and say that that represents the totality of the ray. But I assert an equal untruth, if I say that this white ray does not contain in itself the possibility and potency of the red ray. It is not less than red: it is more; for it contains all the colors of the spectrum. So, when I see personality in myself or you, manifested as one part and outcome of the infinite life of things, I have no right to say that this personality represents the totality of that life. Neither have I a right to say that the totality of that life is not as much as I am. It is infinitely more. So, when I deny personality as an attribute of God, I am not belittling him, I am not taking away something from him, I am not making him smaller and less in dignity and goodness and glory: I am only asserting that personality is a little, feeble, finite, limited word, that cannot sum up the infinite capacity of God. God is unspeakably more than personal. Personality is one of his local, finite manifestations. But is the infinite, that manifests itself as personal, less than its own manifestation? God is unspeakably more than we mean by that word then, while he holds in himself all that is sweet and gracious and tender and hopeful and helpful,— more than that word is accustomed in our thought and speech to cover.

One more thought only on this question of personality.

What is the essence, the essential idea, of personality? It is not outline, it is not limitation, it is not location in space. A rock or a tree is outlined, shaped, located at a particular point. I never think of calling it a person. Why? It lacks that which is really central in our thought as supplying personality. It lacks consciousness, it lacks intelligence, it lacks selfhood. John Locke, the English philosopher, says that the central idea of personality is thought and intelligence. Hermann Lotze, one of the foremost scientific philosophers of the world, asserts the same. Conscious selfhood, he says, is the essence of personality. And so we may assert and believe that God is personal, while we eliminate from the definition of that word all that limits, all that locates, all that cripples, all that hampers personality, as we are acquainted with it in ourselves and in each other. And we may rightly, I believe,— carefully defining terms and understanding what they mean,— assert of God that he is the Infinite Person. Now then, passing this question with this necessary brevity and condensation, and yet covering, I believe, all that is essential, I pass to the third and last point that I shall now offer for your consideration.

Is God good? If he is not, he is not God. Prove whatever else you may concerning him, if we cannot trust him, if we cannot love him, if we cannot put our hand into his, though his is hidden in a cloud, and walk by his side like a little child by the side of his father in the dark, believing that, though we do not know where we are going, he does,— if, I say, we cannot believe that, then for all practical purposes, for our hearts and our hopes, there is no God. Good? What do we mean by that word? What I mean and what I believe the world is coming rapidly to mean, what the world must mean, is this: God, if he be anything, is king over all things, blessed forever. No definition of him can mean anything to us, as being good, unless it means, some time, some when, some where, an outcome of good for every being that thinks and breathes. And so I assert, without fear of contradiction, that in the popular churches of the day God is not defined as a good being. Assert it loudly as they will, the very definition of their theology contains in itself the elements which contradict the assertion, and will echo and shout that contradiction in its face forever. If there is one single human soul that is to suffer torture forever, then God is not good. It implies then an outcome of good for every one of his children. That is what good means.

Now, is God good? Have we any reason, any rational right, to believe that he is good in so grand and so comprehensive a sense as that? What is the indictment that is brought against him? I would that I might at least suggest to you the way by which we may "justify the ways of God to men." I believe with my whole soul that they are justifiable. What is the indictment against God's goodness? A philosopher, a profound thinker, like John Stuart Mill, will sum up the argument for you, and say that all we have a right to do is to place the evils of life on one side of the account-book, and the good on the other, and assert that perhaps there is more of good in God than there is of evil; and yet that there must be both, because both good and evil exist. That is, Mill tells us that we must either limit God's goodness or limit his power. Evil, he says, exists. Then, God does not want to get rid of it, or he cannot. That is his argument. If he does not want to, he is limited in his love or his goodness. If he cannot, he is limited in his power. In either case, he is not the infinite God of whom we are speaking. Let us, then, look at the indictment. What is it? What is it that makes men question whether God is good?

Here, for example, in human experience, are death, sickness, pain, poverty, crime, heartache, tears, all "the ills that flesh is heir to." These make the black indictment that the thought and the heart of humanity bring up against the goodness of God. Either defiantly, or with pain and heartache and tears, men assert: "I would not treat people in that fashion. No father could treat his own child as God treats man. He must be different from anything that we call loving or kind, or such things would not exist."

Now, let us look at the problem just as carefully and as fearlessly as we can for a few moments. First take the one item, death. Is death an evil? It may be; but do we know that it is an evil, so that we have a right, on the score of the existence of death, to assert a lack of love and wisdom and fatherhood on the part of God? I dare assert, without fear of contradiction from any quarter, that we have no such right. I believe that death is not an evil, but a good. It is universal. Some time or other, every one of us must bow and pass through that arched, low, dark gateway out into the beyond, — absolutely universal. If it be an evil, then God is a fiend; for he has put this evil upon the shoulders and the heart of everything that breathes. But I say no man knows that it is an evil; and the heart and hope and trust of the world in all ages have dared to assert, to believe at least, that it is a good, an infinite and unspeakable good. And if that whisper that is in every human soul tell us true,— that death only leads out into something better and higher, that it is a necessary step in human advance,— then it is no more an evil than is birth, which brought us out of the darkness into this wonderful light of life. And I believe that, if death came to us stripped of its accidents, we should never think of it as an evil. When we speak of death, we do not mean the simple act of sleep at last, with a hope of waking up in a higher and better life. That is not what the most of us mean, when we talk about the evil of death. It is premature death, it is painful death, it is horrible death, it is a death of anguish, a death of despair, a death of lingering torture, it is separation, it is ten thousand things grouped about and connected with the fact of dissolution. If death only came to us as it ought to come, after a long life in which we had tasted all the sweets and pleasures of existence, and, like children at night, were tired and wanted to lie down and go to sleep; if death only came to us as the leaves fall from a tree, without any bleeding, any pain, simply taking on their beautiful robes of color and falling silently through the air upon the soft bed of earth,— if death came like that, we should never think of its being an evil: it would be simply going to sleep when we were weary, simply stopping when we got through. And, if it came to us in such guise as this, the simple fact that by the removal of the population of the earth every few years to make place for new-comers whose nerves were again to be thrilled with the joy of life, whose glad eyes were to look upon the bright faces of the stars, whose hearts were to thrill with the music of the wind in the tree-tops and of the waves upon the sea-shore, whose hearts were to rejoice in the love of father, mother, wife, child, and friend, whose brains were to be busied with the great, magnificent, inspiring problems of life,— I say this consideration that thus generation after generation were to come and sit down at this bounteous board of life, and then when they had feasted to sail out sleeping into the beyond,— we should say that death might not be an evil at all, but only a marvellous increment of the world's happiness, distributing that happiness to untold millions instead of confining it to the first-comers, a very few. I believe this to be the true conception of death. All these things that make death hideous, the horrible dreams of the beyond that frighten us, the pains and sorrows and lingering diseases, the mangling accidents that accompany and produce it, — these things, did God make them? No, not one of them! They are all preventable accompaniments of death, and no part of death itself, — things for which we, and we alone, are responsible. Death as God made it, and as it comes to those that live the life of God, is no more horrible than the falling to sleep in my arms of my little girl at night, as I rock her in the twilight. God's death is just sinking off to sleep in God's arms.

Leaving that, then, out of the question for a moment, let us look at this other thing, — I shall have to group them all together, — pain, suffering, disease, poverty, hunger, want, and crime, summed up and put into one account, and that we call evil. And what are they? Are they things that are essential in the conception of this universe? No, not one. They are no part of the necessary laws and life of God. They are every one of them simply the results of human ignorance and perversity breaking those laws. The universe in every part, in all its lawful movement and order, is one grand harmony, beautiful and good; and all evil is simply the result of human ignorance, human passion, human perversity. There is not an evil on the face of the earth that needs to exist.

But still the problem is not settled yet, though we can assert, and assert clearly, that the universe is perfect benevolence toward man. All that we call human civilization is simply man's finding out things that have been true forever, and applying them to his own use. All that we call truth is simply man's discovery of that which has been true from the beginning. They are nothing that he has created or added to the sum of things. All that we call the moral progress of the world is simply man's discovering and obeying the laws of his own being and the laws of the universe, that are eternal. All these tell us, prove beyond the possibility of a question, that the universe in itself is good, is true, is sound, is real, is the friend and helper of man. In every department of the world, in the stars above and the depths beneath us, the world is the storehouse of God, waiting for man to use it. He calls upon the lightning which had played for ages in the clouds, and it runs as his errand-boy. He uses the stars to guide his ships over the fathomless waves. He taps the earth, and calls out the imprisoned and imbedded sunlight buried there thousands of years ago, to kindle the flames in his grate, and to illuminate his nights in his dwellings and along his streets. Every mountain is a treasure-house, every field a store of wealth. It only needs that man ask intelligently for the things he needs, and this eternal overflowing fulness of God is ready bountifully to supply every one.

But I said a moment ago the question is not settled yet. Perhaps that which is the most central and important of them all remains. Though the universe outside of man be good, and though it be possible for men to live a life here that is free from all that we call evil, if God really loved man and wanted him to be happy, why did he not create him so that he would live rightly? There is the central, crucial question of all. If God is a father of love, of wisdom, and wants man to be happy, why did he not create him so that he would be? Why did he not give him wisdom enough to know, at the start, everything that he has found out in these long and weary centuries? Why did he not give him power to control nature, to obey all its laws, knowledge to understand them all, so that he might ward off poverty and want and disease and pain and suffering of every kind? Let us think for a moment now, and think very carefully.

This resolves itself into another question, a question no less than this: as to which is better, that man should have been created an automaton, a perfect machine, or a being who should progressively learn things by experience. That is what the question means. A man can make a machine in the shape of a child, and so support it, this side and that, that it shall go through the process of walking, and never fall as long as it exists. A child stumbles and falls and hurts itself at every turn, while learning to walk. Is the machine better than the child, because it never stumbles or gets hurt? Babbage, the great mathematician, could make a "calculating machine" that should never make a mistake in working out mathematical problems. Young Newton, who was to tower like a god of intellect over all the possible mathematical machines that science could ever frame, blundered and stumbled at every turn in learning the multiplication-table,— the first rudiments of the figures with which he was to outline the movements of the stars at the last. You go to Italy, and they will construct you a hand-organ so perfectly that it shall be incapable of making a mistake in playing a tune. Mozart, Beethoven, the great musicians, the master-minds of the world, blundered and stumbled at every step in fingering the keys with unused hands, and feeling their way out through the marvellous mazes and intricacies of musical law and sound. We can construct a machine that, using the sun, shall give you a perfect photograph of the face or a landscape. But the artists Angelo, Titian, Rubens, the great artists of the world, experimented and daubed and labored for years before they attained the power of creating the masterpieces that alone are worthy to be called art.

I say then, it is a question as to which is better: that God should have made man an intelligent, self-acting machine, never to make a mistake, never to feel hurt, never to be conscious of wrong, never to stumble to rise again, or that he should make him what he is, a being learning from experience, progressing by attempts and trials. Which, think you, is the grander? And, if man is to learn progressively by experience, he must perforce make mistakes, he must stumble, he must hurt himself against the sharp corners of things, he must overstep laws, and find that fire burns, that cold freezes, and that hunger kills. He thus learns to keep within the limits of these marvellous, invisible laws of life, and thus he becomes a free-born king, a child of God, and not a machine. And if, friends,— and no man knows enough to deny it,— if it be true, as we hope and dare to believe, that man by this experience is being fitted for a grander and larger life beyond, that he is to outgrow, slough off, and tread under foot the imperfections and faults of his being, as the child ceases to stumble and to make mistakes and comes to be a man; if, I say, we by and by are to reach up and blossom out into this perfect, grand, glorious manhood,— become the sons and daughters of God,— then our life, however much of suffering or pain there is in it, is not only justified, it is glorified; and it stands no longer as an impeachment of the goodness of God; it may be even the very crowning manifestation of his goodness.

I believe then, that in the true use of language, remembering that it is symbolical and only shadows forth the infinite reality, we may say that we can rationally believe that God is conscious, personal, and good. And, however much of doubt or difficulty may still surround us, we may close with the song of hope which has been so beautifully sung by Whittier: —

> "Within the maddening maze of things,
> And tossed by storm and flood,
> To one fixed stake my spirit clings.
> *I know that God is good!*"

Why Does God not Reveal Himself?

Our subject this morning is the question as to why God does not reveal himself to men, so as to set all our great puzzling questions at rest. Why are we left to doubt, to discuss, and to dispute? Why is not everything made clear?

If you open any book dealing with Christian doctrine or Christian evidences written during the last hundred years, you will be quite sure to find that it starts out with the assumption that, given an intelligent, personal God, who cares anything about man, a revelation of himself may be confidently expected. And, since the persons who have been engaged in elaborating these schemes of doctrine and evidence knew of no book more likely to contain that revelation than the one we call the Bible, the next assumption which naturally follows is that the Bible is this revelation. Without stopping to take your time in dealing with this second assumption, I wish to say that I perfectly agree with the first one. If there be a God, intelligent, conscious, loving, our Father, one who cares for the race, we have a right to expect that he will reveal himself to us. But right here, on the very threshold of our discussion, there are two or three points that we must notice for clearness of thought and as bearing on the farther development of our theme.

In the first place, it is confidently assumed by most writers and speakers on this subject that we may not only expect a revelation, but that we may expect and that we need an infallible revelation. Now, I wish distinctly to say that I for one do not believe that there is the slightest necessity for an infallible revelation on religious subjects any more than on any other subject whatsoever; that is, unless God is a being who will eternally damn his own children for intellectual mistakes, after they have done the best they possibly can in the circumstances to find out the truth,— I say, unless God is that kind of a being, we do not need an infallible religious revelation any more than we need an infallible scientific or artistic or industrial revelation.

Furthermore, not only do we not need an infallible revelation, but any such revelation seems to me to be an absurdity, an impossibility in the nature of things. Consider for a moment what it implies. It is not a question as to whether God can infallibly utter himself: it is a question as to whether fallible men can infallibly listen, infallibly interpret, infallibly report. It may be ever so infallible on the divine side; but, until men are something more than fallible, it cannot be free from error on the human side. I may utter myself ever so clearly to a child. The child can only take what the childish mind is capable of appreciating and understanding. Newton may talk for a year to a North American Indian. The Indian cannot possibly comprehend his *Principia;* and what he does comprehend he may misinterpret. He may report incorrectly the next time that he tells one of his neighbors what Newton said to him. He may have forgotten a part of it, he may have added something which was not in the original statement. A thousand sources of error are open in every direction.

Still another point. If you will think of it, it is absurd and impossible in the nature of things for an infinite, boundless, absolute being to reveal himself as infinite, as boundless, as absolute, to a finite and limited nature. It is not a question as to whether God would like to reveal himself to man as he is and all he is: it is a question of possibility. The omnipotent cannot commit that which is absurd and impossible. Omnipotence itself cannot make a square without four sides to it. Omnipotence itself cannot make a stick without two ends. Omnipotence itself cannot make two mountains without a valley between them. Omnipotence cannot be absurd; and so the infinite, I say, as infinite, cannot be revealed to the finite. Suppose a man attempts to reveal to me, while I am in the centre of the continent, the Atlantic Ocean: what will he do? He will try perhaps a verbal description. But, unless I have seen the ocean, the words cannot mean to me what they mean to the speaker. Suppose he brings me a bucketful of water from the Atlantic: has he revealed to me the ocean? It is only a bucket of water, no matter where it came from. He is confined by the limits of the method he uses in which to reveal it to me. So the infinite cannot possibly reveal itself as infinite to the finite. It can only manifest itself in limited, confined ways, with broken lights and fragmentary utterances.

But another point. Men say, If the Bible is not infallible, or if something is not infallible, if we have not an infallible revelation somewhere, how, then, are we to know what is truth? In the first place I remark, in answer to this inquiry, that concerning a great many things that men are very anxious to find out it does not make any special, practical difference whether they know what is truth or not. Concerning any question of the world that is not to-day accessible and verifiable, it does not make any great or important difference whether we can find out the truth about it or not. Men are very much exercised over the authorship of the **poems** of Homer. It is of no great practical importance to the nineteenth century whether the man who wrote Homer spelled his name with five letters or with eight, whether he lived in one city or in another city. And I carry this principle even so far as touching the life and doctrines of Jesus Christ himself. Even if it were proved to me that no such man as Jesus ever lived or ever spoke, it would not touch by the weight of a hair one of the great practical principles by which to-day I seek to live, and in the light of which I hope to die. We lay much more stress on these things that we cannot find out and settle than we are justified in doing. It would not make honesty dishonest, it would not make purity impure, kindness unkind. It would not touch, I say, the great underlying principles of your life. How do we find out what is true, then? Why, we have the only means that any man ever had in the world, or ever will have. We find out what is true and what is good by the practical experience of man. How do you find out whether a thing is white or black? No one has any special difficulty in detecting the difference between sugar and vinegar. We can tell whether a thing is gold or brass. We can tell whether an object is beautiful or ugly. And so in regard to the great principles of life. They have, the world over, to be tested ultimately by human experience; and there is no other possible way of testing them. Those things are good that experience has found to be good for man: those things are evil that experience has found to be injurious to man. There is no special trouble, then, in regard to deciding what is right and what is wrong, what is good and what is evil. And, even if we had a revelation that was declared to be infallible, it would not help us one whit. The only way by which we could find out ultimately as to whether the revelation was correct or not would be by human experience. If we bring a revelation to the test, this is the one final, ultimate, and only test. Men always have done it. Whether they have been clear in their thinking as to what they were about or not, they always will do it, they always must do it.

Now, then, let us look for a moment at this question of the possibility of God's revealing himself to men in any one of the ways that have been popular in the legendary, mythologic thought of the world. I take it that, for the most part, men and women assume, without any very careful thought on the subject, that God might reveal himself to us infallibly and put these subjects beyond question, if he chose, in any one of a dozen ways. In order to clarify our thought, then, on this subject, we will look at a few of the different methods that have been thought about by men. And, in the first place, take the method of incarnation. Suppose God should decide to come to the world in the form of a man, could he in that way give us an infallible revelation of himself? Why, what would he be when he got here? They tell us in regard to Jesus, in order to explain the limitation of his being, that God shore himself of his glory, that he put off his omnipotence, that he dispensed for the time being with his omniscience, that he humbled himself and became in the form of a man. Grant it for a moment. What have we then, when God has ceased to be God in all his fulness and completeness, for the sake of being a man? He is not God any longer: he is a man. Precisely parallel to the idea that I spoke of a moment ago, concerning the attempt to transfer the Atlantic to the Mississippi Valley in a bucket. It is not the Atlantic: it is a bucket of water. Or, if God leaves his omnipotence and his infinity and his eternity, and takes on the limitations and form of a man, he cannot possibly by so doing reveal his Godhood: the utmost that he can reveal is the perfection of manhood, for he has become a man. There is, then, no revelation of God here that transcends or reaches beyond the limits of perfect humanity.

Take another supposition. Suppose God should decide to infallibly inspire a prophet to reveal his will. The only way by which we should know that this revelation through the prophet was infallible would be by the test of human experience that I have just spoken about. If the prophet should say that he was infallibly inspired, it would be open to any man to question as to whether his testimony was valid. He might be perfectly honest, and still be mistaken. There would be no possible way that I can conceive of by which he should put the matter beyond question. And, even if he did give us a revelation, it would be only to those persons that received it at first hand. It would be human tradition, very human, possibly very faulty, as we have found in all instances the wide world over, just the moment it passed beyond the lips of the individual prophet himself.

Suppose again that God should decide to speak to the world out of a clear heaven over our heads, and declare to men his existence and reveal to them his characteristics: he must speak in some one human language. It would be a message only to those that heard. This message would have to be translated by fallible men into other languages. It would be only human testimony, human tradition to the next generation and all the future ages of the world, liable to ten thousand misconceptions, mistranslations, and misstatements of every kind. There is a report in the New Testament that is instructive in its suggestiveness in regard to this matter. It is said that on a certain occasion a great light shone upon a certain man, and that a voice spoke to him out of the light. And it is also said in this immediate connection that some of the people there saw the form of somebody, but did not hear anything; and some of the rest of them heard the voice, but saw nothing. On another occasion, when it is said that a voice out of the sky spoke to Jesus himself, there did not seem to be any agreement on the part of the listeners. Some of them said it thundered only; some of them said it was the divine voice. It is absurd to suppose that in any such way as this there could be the possibility of an infallible revelation. What would it mean to us to-day if the report came to us from a hundred years ago that somebody in Europe heard the voice of God out of heaven speaking to him? No sane man would believe it. It at any rate would be open to most serious question. We should have to rely upon his accuracy of hearing as to what the voice said, upon his wisdom, upon his judgment. It would not be, in other words, the infallible voice of God, but only human testimony as to what a fallible man supposed he heard.

Take again that other supposition, that God should write a book. Suppose God did write one with his own finger,— only he would have to assume a finger for the occasion; that is, he would have to limit himself, bring himself down to the level of a man, in order to do it. But suppose he did it,— that he wrote an absolutely infallible book. He would have to write it in some one of the many languages of the world. It would have to be translated into the rest, and would be liable to misinterpretation and mistranslation in every form. Suppose he should write it at the same time in all the languages of the world. Any one who is at all familiar with this subject knows that languages are perpetually being born and languages are dying, just like members of the human race. And, if he had written it in the English language of Chaucer's time, we could not read it to-day without translation. And, furthermore, human language itself is a fallible medium for the carrying of ideas. There is no possibility, I suppose, that any living man could put into language his ideas on any possible subject in such a way that that language should bear one meaning, and only one.

Here are commentators by the thousand, to-day, fighting not only over the Bible, but over Shakespeare,— not only over what he wrote, but as to what he meant by what all admit that he wrote. There is no possible word that conveys one shade of meaning, and only one. And, when you have a phrase that may mean any one of half a dozen different things, let it be ever so infallible as it issues from God, how shall we know which one of the six possible meanings it shall bear? The giving to the world, then, an infallible revelation by a book, if you trace it through and see what it means, is an absurdity on the face of it. Look at the Bible itself. Suppose, for a moment, that it is infallible; and then look at the hundreds and thousands of different readings. Look at the sects arrayed in deadly battle against each other,— one of them fighting for what he believes to be God's truth, on the interpretation of a little text, and building a whole sect on it; another believing that the first is an emissary of the devil because he gives it that interpretation, and he building another sect on the other side of the same text. It is simply impossible that there should be an infallible revelation given to men in any such way.

Once more, suppose that God, by an interposition of miraculous power, should write his name across the sky in letters of stars; should declare thus that God is; that he loves men; that he desires them to do so and so. This, again, would have to be in some one special language of the world. It would have to be translated and interpreted to all the rest of the nations. Or, if it were written in all the different languages of the world, the meaning of words changes from age to age, as I have already told you. People a few hundred years from now would not be able to read it. And then, again, it would be open to any man to question as to whether the supposed purposed arrangement of stars did not take place under precisely the same law that arranges them in their present wonderful order. The formation of crystals of frost on your window-panes is just as wonderful as would be any other arrangement of those same crystals that should make them spell out letters and words.

Again, suppose God should attempt to attract the devotion of the world by a series of stupendous miracles. Suppose these miracles occurred to-day. The next generation would have to take the fact of their occurrence on our testimony; and the chances are that, if they were wise, they would not believe a word about it. Again, consider the thoughts that would spring up out of the occurrence of these stupendous miracles. The question would at once arise as to whether the same God, who is accustomed to work through the orderly arrangement of the world, was the one who was disturbing and upsetting this orderly arrangement,—the question whether there were not two gods, one of them wiser and better than the other, one of them trying to keep things in order and the other to disturb it. For, if God is doing right in the present arrangement of the world, if he is doing the best, any change in that right or best could only be a change of that right and best to the relatively wrong; and this miraculous disturbance would upset the confidence and destroy the possibility of knowledge on the part of civilization. A revelation of this kind, then, is absurd.

And now, having reviewed thus briefly all these different conceivable ways and found them wanting in some one essential element of infallibility, where are we left? Are we stranded on the shore of the impossibility of God's speaking to man at all? No: I believe that God has spoken to man, and that he is speaking to-day; and that, in the very nature of things, being a living and working God, he must speak to every intelligence that is competent to understand the symbols by which he utters his thoughts and his laws. God has given man a revelation,— a revelation in two volumes: volume first, the physical laws and life of the universe; and volume second, the nature and history and aspiration and hopes and struggles of man. Physical nature and man are the perpetual, the living, the progressive, the ever-unfolding revelation of God. God has revealed himself as existing, as the one, as the infinite, as the eternal, as intelligent, as conscious, as personal,— in the sense I have given to that word,— as good, as the father and friend of man. Look over the leaves, for a moment, of this magnificent revelation, and see some of the things therein contained. The greatness of God: his grandeur is manifested in the stars, the depths, the infinite depths of the heavens over our heads; and then, even in this world, the might and the majesty of mountains, the grandeur of oceans, the perilous magnificence of avalanches, the precipitous heights and mountainous valleys, like the Yosemite; the thunderous grandeur of cataracts, like Niagara; the overpowering greatness that thrusts itself upon us at every turn, and awes us with the fulness of the majesty of this being of which even these things are only whispers, while we are compelled to say, The greatness, "the thunders of his power, who can understand?" In the placid brightness of the moon walking across the silvery night sky, the sheen of the waters under the glancing rays of the sun, the beautiful tinting of the unfolding rose, the more beautiful tinting of a maiden's cheek, the deep, unfathomable beauty of a little child's eye, the grace of the locks of hair that fall over their foreheads; this instinct of beauty in man that creates wonderful statues out of stone, and covers canvas with the creations of his thought; all this infinite beauty of the world,— the music of bird-songs, the beauty of the plumage of the bird of paradise, the wondrous and artistic finish of the humming-bird's wing, beauty in the heavens above and in the earth beneath,— only a little glinting and shadowing forth of the infinite beauty that is deep in the heart of the universe, and shines out as a flash of the glory of God. And then the love of God, manifested in the infinite bounty of the universe on every hand; welling up in the feelings of friendship; incarnate in the mother bending over the cradle of her child or watching through hours of silent agony day after day, night after night; the love that binds husband and wife together, and creates all the beauty and happiness of the world; the devotion witnessed to by martyr fires, by the heroic struggles and toils and travels and battles for humanity and for the right; the pity, the tenderness, and charity of men like Wilberforce, of men like Howard, of men like our own heroic Garrison,— men that cared and suffered and dared for men they had never seen and never would see; for those that were criminal, shut up, by the hand of justice, in prison; for those that would never learn to lisp their name or pay them one iota of gratitude,— all these things, simply little glints and gleamings and outshinings of the infinite life of this universe, whispering what it can never utter, the unspeakable, the unutterable reserve that is ever behind!

This universe then,— all its essential laws a revelation of God's truth, all its beauty a revelation of God's taste, all its heroism and devotion and kindness and charity a revelation of God's love,— this universe, then,— nature and man, these two volumes,— is the one book of God, and the only book that God has ever written. All truth is a part of this book, whether in Christianity or Buddhism, whether in America or the heart of Africa, whether in the stars or the earth, whether in science or religion, whether among the brutes or among men. Whatever is true is a letter, a syllable, a phrase, a sentence, of the writing of this book of God. Whatever is untrue,— whether it fell from the lips of Jesus or Buddha, whether it be in Christian Bible or Hindoo Bible or African fetichism,— whatever is untrue is a misreading, a mistranslation, a misinterpretation of the one, magnificent, only book of God. All the Bibles that were ever written were only attempts, partial attempts, to transcribe the infinite and eternal truth. And it seems to me not only absurd, but impious, if men understood its implication, to claim that a book written centuries ago, when the world was barbaric, when ninety-nine hundredths of the modern knowledge of civilization was unknown,— a book written nobody knows where, nobody knows when, nobody knows by whom, for the most part,— I say it seems to me not only absurd, but impious, for men to thrust this upon us, and say, Here is the book and the only book of God; and you are impious and rebellious against God, when you prefer the whole to a feeble attempt to transcribe a part. For this infinite book of God does not exclude Christianity, does not exclude Jesus, does not exclude the Bible: it includes all that the experience of the race has verified, or ever shall verify as true, and subsumes it as a part in its magnificent generalization. This, then, is the book of God, the only conceivable revelation that could be made to man,— a book written in letters, a part of which every intelligence can read. And that is the only possibility concerning any book that ever was written. It can be read just as fast and as far as human intelligence rises to the height of its magnificent meaning.

Now, then, let us glance over for a moment, one after another, a few of the main characteristics of this revelation. This revelation of God in physical nature and in man is in itself an infallible revelation. But, as I said at the opening of my discourse, it, equally with any other book, must be liable to error and mistranslation and misinterpretation on our part. Infallible in itself, it must forever be fallible to us, because we can never be absolutely certain that, in this particular or that, we may not have made a more or less serious mistake. And yet it contains all truth; and as fast as we are able to read it, as far as we are able to verify its statements, we shall have attained all the infallibility that is possible, all the infallibility that is desirable.

The next characteristic of this word of God is that it is an oracle never silent. In the words of the Psalm which I read as our lesson this morning, "Day uttereth speech unto day, and night showeth knowledge unto night. There is no speech nor language where their voice is not heard. Their line has gone out into all the earth, and their words to the end of the world." That is, God at the same moment speaks in every language, speaks to every race, speaks to every man, and speaks just as much of his truth as the man physically, intellectually, morally, and spiritually is capable of comprehending. It is not a Bible that depends upon any one person's translation, or a translation made at any one time. It is not a Bible depending upon tradition, it is not a Bible depending upon human testimony. This word of God spoke a hundred thousand years ago, and with the same unerring voice it speaks to-day. To-day any man may listen, he may listen to-night, he may hear it to-morrow. It will speak through the next hundred thousand years, it will utter itself forever. A Bible then, is this, not depending upon the translation of any one man, upon the testimony of any one man or group of men, upon the tradition of any one man or group of men,— a Bible whose language never becomes obsolete, never is outworn, never is capable of being misrepresented by one man to another in such a way that he cannot correct the error.

Another characteristic of this Bible is that it is progressive in its revelations. All of God's truth, all of God's life, is here; but it unfolds itself like a scroll of parchment, such as men used to read, to keep step, age after age, with the progress of human intelligence and human need. We can read to-day all we need to know to-day for the practical carrying on of our life. To-morrow, we can read all that we shall need to know for to-morrow. And here is one thing, if you will allow me by way of parenthesis to stop and impress it upon you, that I would like to say. One great source of all the miseries of the world is just here: instead of men busily engaging themselves in doing those things that are practical and necessary for to-day, to make the world what it ought to be to-day, they neglect these present duties, scattered loosely all about their feet, while they muse and speculate over things that as yet it is not possible for them to know, and that would be of no practical value, if it were. We know enough to-day to lay the foundations here in Boston of the veritable kingdom of God. We know enough to-day here in Boston to sweep out of existence literally nine-tenths of the evils under which humanity suffers. But these things, for the most part, we are neglecting, while we dream and speculate and quarrel as to whether we are to know our friends in the future life, or whether we are to be encased in bodies or to flit about as intangible ghosts,— matters impossible for us to settle, and of no practical use to us, if we could settle them.

Another characteristic of this revelation is what I have already more than once hinted at in the course of my discussion. It is a revelation adequate to all our needs. It gives us information, and all the information that is necessary, concerning all the great practical questions of life. There is no one single thing that you need to know in order to live the noblest manly and womanly life about which there is any serious practical discussion. They are speculative matters that you are doubting about and troubling yourself over.

The last characteristic that I shall ask you to notice is that this revelation not only is not finished, but in the nature of things never will be, and never can be finished. It is a revelation unfolding age after age, keeping step with the progress of human intelligence, and determined by that intelligence. And, if you will think of it for a moment, you will be put at rest concerning many of the problems that have perplexed and troubled you. Why does not God reveal to me the things that are beyond the present experience of the world? Perhaps you assume that he might, if he chose; that it is a mere arbitrary drawing of the veil on the part of our Father in heaven. And perhaps, moreover, you wonder why it is, whether he really is willing to tell us. Do you know you are asking an absurdity? You are asking an impossibility. What does knowledge mean? It has no meaning whatever, except as it generalizes the results of human experience. We know, and can know, only what the world has found out by experience; for that is what knowledge means. There is no possibility of knowing anything beyond that experience. Let me refer to the old and often used illustration of our relation to a child, that I may make this perfectly clear; for I believe it to be very important. I take my child, seven years of age, and I try with all the power of language that I possess to make clear to her what something means that is years ahead of her experience. I am engaged in something that is absurd, useless, a waste of time. I may put it into ever so clear words: she cannot possibly comprehend what they mean. Suppose we are sailing out in a ship over an unknown and heretofore untraversed sea. Why, of course the only way that I can know what there is a hundred miles ahead of me is by sailing over that hundred miles and finding out. There is no other possible way. Suppose God should attempt to put it into human language, into the English language, into the ordinary speech of Boston, what the future life, what heaven means. He might give a perfectly adequate expression to it, but it would be utter jargon to us; for there is no possible way by which we can apprehend an idea that transcends the bounds and limits of human experience. Suppose a man should come back from travelling in a foreign land, and try to explain to you something the like of which you never heard of or saw. Do you not see the absurdity of the undertaking? You ask him what shape it had, and he would tell you it was not in the shape of anything that you ever saw. What color was it? Why, it was an absolutely new color, not at all like any color you ever saw in your life. And so on concerning one after another of its characteristics. If he should tell you that it was not at all like anything you have ever seen, why, when he got through, no matter how long he talked, he would have simply told you nothing. And so if the future, the higher life,—granting its existence,—be utterly and entirely unlike anything that our experience has made us acquainted with up to this hour, then it is not an arbitrary drawing of the veil for God to hide the future. It is an impossibility that the veil should be drawn by any other than our own human hands. This revelation, then, will never be finished. It will keep step with our own experience and progress. And it will have that pleasing, luring mystery about it that makes us ever desire to walk on and on, and to see what of glory and greatness is in store for us in the future. And this is not a calamity: it is a marvellous blessing. When I know how a story is coming out, I do not want to read it any more. If I knew eternity already, it would be a weary, tedious task to walk through the ages. I should want to lie down and sink into an endless sleep. This revelation, then, will never be finished; and, thank God, it never can be. We will read a new leaf every day, a new book every century; and it will still have wonder-tales and glorious truths for us forever and forever.

SHALL WE WORSHIP GOD?

It is a fact so notorious as to need on my part not argument nor proof, but only mention, that the popular feeling concerning the subject of worship is such that many men and women, the truest and best of the time, shrink from it as something not quite worthy of the noblest and most dignified manhood and womanhood. The very word calls up the thought of a cringing, half-whining, unmanly attitude toward God. It is associated in the thought of many with rituals and ceremonies that seem to them to have no vitality, no real meaning; and so they come to feel that they cannot heartily enter into that which is accustomed to go by the name of worship. And, mark you, as I have already intimated, this is not because these men are not true, because they are not honest, because they are not earnest, not devoted to all those things that make up in the popular estimate a noble, sweet, true, faithful life. A part of this feeling, I think, springs by way of reaction out of the very intensity of these noble and manly qualities. There is a feeling that when they are called to go to church and engage in worship they are somehow surrendering something of that which they have come to regard as noblest and best in their nature; they are asked to do something that they feel their very manliness forbids.

And then, on the other hand, these same people have a very serious question deep down in their hearts as to whether there is any being in the universe that wants them to do anything of the sort; a question as to whether, if God exists, he is a being who cares whether they get down on their knees or not, whether they bow their head in the attitude of prayer, whether they read the prescribed ritual and scripture of the day from the prayer-book, whether they engage in those things that are customarily called worship; and then a feeling stronger than this,— and which I must confess to you I heartily share,— as to whether, if God really wants them to flatter in the common terms of adulation, they can have any true, deep, hearty respect for him. We are accustomed to feel that those are not the noblest types of men who are pleased with fulsome flattery. They are not the noblest types of men who care the most for the shouts and the hat-waving of the crowd; who are pleased to stand up and have an oration delivered to them, telling them how great and how noble and how fine they are. He who really deserves these things, we rather feel, shrinks from this public expression of them. A gentleman, not long since, talking with a friend of mine, gave outright and common expression to this feeling,— one that I doubt not large numbers of you will sympathize with, — when he said in his plain, familiar fashion, "If there is any God in heaven, he must have a queer idea of the people who think they can please him by continually telling him how big he is." He can have no very great respect for men who think that it is real worship, something that he desires, for them to be engaged in this fulsome adulation.

I say this, in some rough sort of fashion, sets forth a very common, wide-spread feeling in the community. In order that we may understand the subject and see what relation this sort of thing called worship bears to that which is genuine, we need at the very outset to start with a definition. What is worship? What is it to worship anything? Above all things, What is it to worship God? If we take the sentiment that goes by this name and analyze it carefully until we come to the feeling that lies at its heart, that gives it color and power and meaning, we shall, I think, discover that the one element that all genuine worship has in common is the feeling that we call admiration. A man worships that which he admires, whether it be below him or above him, whatever name he call it by, or whether he give it any verbal or formal expression or not. And in however many creeds he may write it down, through how many formalities soever he may pass, whatever he may say or do, a man does not worship that which he does not heartily and earnestly admire. Worship, then, is admiration. Let us keep that one definition in mind, and let it run all through our discussion, linking the different parts of it together, and, like a line of light, illuminating it all.

And what is the tendency of this feeling of worship? What is its power over the heart and life of the worshipper? The very definition that I have given you carries in its heart the answer to this question. A man instinctively and inevitably tends to become like, to become assimilated to, that which he really admires. To use a Biblical expression, "Beholding as in a glass the glory of the Lord, we are changed into the same image." If a man really admires and worships that glory, he is transformed into its likeness, changed from glory to glory, day by day assimilating himself to it more and more. As an illustration of what I mean in its practical bearing on life and conduct, take the case of Alexander the Great. It is said that the one book that he cared for above all others in the world was Homer's *Iliad;*

and that the one character in all that book that impressed him, that became his ideal, was the character of Achilles. He slept with this poem under his pillow, and dreamed about it by day. It was the star that led him through his long campaigns from Greece to the depths of Asia. And the natural result followed. Worshipping this ideal warrior, he, day by day, consciously or unconsciously, modelled and moulded his life after the pattern of the Grecian hero. On the other hand, let a man take the ideal saint of the Catholic Church as his model; let the one book that he shall read be *The Imitation of Christ*, by à Kempis; let him sleep with that under his pillow; let him carry it about his person, read snatches of it day by day, see in that one ideal wrapped up all the glory, the beauty, the greatness, the grandeur of human life,— and it needs no prophecy to tell what course of action he will pursue; it needs no wise foresight to indicate the position he will occupy next year or in ten years. He becomes inevitably transformed into the likeness of that which he worships. Precisely the same is true if it be some thoroughly ignoble thing. Let a woman care more than for anything else for the position that she occupies in fashionable society. It may not be anything evil in itself; but let this be the supreme object of her worship, the one thing that she admires more than everything else. She may go to church every Sunday in the year; she may read her prayer-book every day; she may attend all the festivals and feasts and days of Lent and the Easter and the Christmas services; she may devote herself to all this external ceremonial, and may think that she is worshipping God. But so long as this is the one thing that she really, deep down in her heart, cares for more than for anything else, she inevitably becomes transformed into this likeness; and, whether she recognizes it or not, those that know her will recognize that she is becoming no larger, no grander, no tenderer, no deeper, no truer than the ideal which is really her God.

Precisely the same thing holds true in every direction. I need not enlarge upon it. If I could become intimately acquainted with the character of any one of you here this morning, I need not ask you what you worship. I need not ask you whether you worship God or not, or whether your worship be in the other direction. I should know from what you are what that one ideal is which you have learned most of all to admire. And if I can see on the part of any one of you a beginning to think and to study, to reach out toward, care for, aspire after something higher and better than you are to-day, if I can see what that thing is, and know that there clings about it something of the beauty, something of the truth, something of the goodness of God, that it is an ideal above you, and that you are really reaching out after it earnestly, I need no prophet to tell me what you will become in the years that are before you. I know by a law as inevitable as that of gravitation that you will become gradually transformed into the image of that which is the object of your worship.

Now, then, for a little more clearness in regard to this religious worship and its nature, let us look at two or three of the common things that are supposed pre-eminently to constitute the worship of God, and see whether they do or not. It is very common for ministers in the pulpit, as they are beginning the office of public prayer, to ask the people to join with them in worship. A man who engages in private prayer in his own closet thinks of himself as worshipping God. If a family group in the morning or the evening gather together to read over some sacred words from one or another scripture, and then kneel down together and unite in their supplications, as they have been trained and habituated to do from the years of their childhood up, they suppose themselves engaged in worshipping God. But, in the light of the definition that we have already given, it is pertinent and important for us to raise the question as to whether they are worshipping God. Persons pray under the impulse of fear; they pray because of habit; they pray from a sense of duty; they pray that they may ward off some supposed possible evil that is likely to come to them in the future; they pray from very selfishness, that they may gain something at the hand of God that they think will not be given to them on any other conditions. Now, in any of these cases, if this be all, or if any one of these principles be pre-eminent, then there will not be connected with this act of prayer the slightest shadow of a shade of worship. It may not be worship at all: it may be even an offence and an abomination in the sight of Him who cares not for the outward expression, but for the reality at the heart.

Or take the public church and temple services of the world in their totality. Churches, in popular language, are called houses of worship. Temples are houses of worship. People gather together on their feast days, their fast days, their new moons, their sabbaths, their holy days of any kind, and unite, as they say, in public worship. But are they worshipping God in any of these ceremonials through which they are passing? The answer depends. It depends entirely upon this very question as to whether this outward ceremonial is the outward expression on their part of a real admiration for that which is divine; or whether, as in the case of the prayer, it be a habit, it be for the sake of gaining something at the hand of God, it be not the impulse of fear or the mere expression of selfishness.

And so in regard to the public processions of religion. Suppose you go to Rome on one of the most important feast days of their year; and the streets are all alive, for to-day the Pope himself appears in procession, accompanied by hundreds of the priesthood and cardinals and dignitaries of the Church; and the people, while the figure, the image of Christ, the *bambino*, passes by, fall down on their faces in the dust. Is this worship? It may be, and it may not. And so when the Jews came from all over Palestine to Jerusalem to engage in what they called their temple-worship,— let it be the feast of tabernacles or of harvest,— gathering there by thousands, meeting early in the morning at the time of the sunrise to chant their songs of praise, meeting again for their elaborate ceremonials and rituals,— the whole city alive with this great jubilee,— on these feast days of religion are the people engaged in worship? Perhaps they are, perhaps not. The whole question here depends upon whether they really worship God in their hearts, whether they really admire him, or are only engaged in external diplomacy, carrying out habits of action, endeavoring to appease his wrath or act upon his inclinations toward them to induce him to grant them some great national favor. It may be no more worship than is that of the man who goes to Washington, and fawns and plans and plots through days and weeks and months to gain the ear of some favorite of him who is highest in power, that he may bring to pass something of benefit to himself or a friend, or the town of which he is a citizen. He may in his heart even despise the very man on whom he fawns, and before whom he gets down in humiliation that he may win his favor.

And so in regard to the great acts and lives of ascetics in the past. Simeon Stylites, standing by the year upon his pillar,— was he worshipping God, or was he winning the plaudits of the multitude, hoping some day to be called a saint, to be looked up to himself, and to be worshipped rather than to worship God? It is the answer to this question that decides whether this form of asceticism or another is real worship or whether it is not. And so in regard to the great public sacrifices of religion,— the holocausts, the burnt offerings, the giving of flowers or fruits or animals,— the offering them up with incense to the God of heaven; or those other sacrifices in our own human lives, when we fast during Lent, when we give up that which we desire, because religion or a priest or public opinion or society bids us do so,— are these things worship of God, again? Hold them up in the clear flame of our definition of worship, as I have given it to you, and see what the color of the deed may be. There is no worship, except that which is a feeling or an expression of sincere admiration for that which is the object of worship.

Worship may or may not be expressed. There may be simply this transient feeling in the heart, which passes away as feeling or which silently thrills and lifts the life, making the man himself feel stronger, purer, nobler, better. Though his lip may not have moved, though this feeling may not have uttered itself in one single bodily movement or habit of any kind, yet, if there be this simple, genuine feeling of admiration for that which is above us, then there is in the heart, so far as it goes, true, sincere worship of God. And yet, if there be this genuine sentiment of admiration, if it be strong within us, if it abide with us day by day and be not simply a flitting, transient feeling that comes and goes, then it will of necessity find for itself external utterance. A man will speak, and he cannot help speaking his worship. A man will live, and he cannot help living out his worship. It may not utter itself in rituals, it may not utter itself through the prescribed channels that are popular at the time; but, if the man be a genuine, day-by-day worshipper of that which is true and noble, it must shape his character, shape his deeds, shape his utterances, and so become visible in some external forms, whether those forms be the same ones week by week or whether they vary infinitely, according to the changing circumstances of life.

It follows then — and here is the important point for us to notice — that if worship be the genuine admiration of the heart and not any external form or uttered word, — it follows, I say, that many persons may really be worshippers of God who think they are not. I meet a great many men, first and last, who would make no sort of claim to being religious. They are dominated by some traditional definition of religion. They think it means going to church, or going to church regularly, or going in some prescribed way; that it means caring about certain sacred days, about certain sacred books; that it means the ability to talk in the prescribed religious or sacred speech of the time; that it means something formal, something that to them has become only an externality with the life all gone out. They reject these things. They are not accustomed to engage in public, perhaps not by outward utterance of word in even private, prayer. They are not accustomed to do anything that goes in the churches by the name of worship, and so they fancy that they are not worshippers; that here is a whole department of human life from which they, by some peculiarity of their nature, are excluded. Now, it may be that a person like this has estimated himself correctly, — that he is not a worshipper. It may be that he does not admire those things that are divine, those things that are godlike, that are above him, that lift and inspire the noblest thoughts of the world. But it does not at all follow that he is not religious, that he is not a sincere worshipper, because he, in the light of the popular definition of the time, fancies that he is not. He may be a man who genuinely loves his home; a man who worships the ideal of womanhood in the wife that he has learned to love; a man whose heart is thrilled and touched by all the beautiful ways of the children about his feet; who sees in them the mystery of this strange and unknown thing, so familiar, so infinite, so unfathomable, that we call life; he may be touched by the beautiful things of the world about him, may pause and gather even a small grass-blade by the roadside, in a walk, and think, until this frail, tiny thing takes him out on an excursion into the infinite, and he stands awestruck and wondering before this mystery of the world; the sight of a wee flower may, as it used to in the case of Wordsworth, touch him even to tears; he may find his soul thrilled and swelling at the tones of the waves on the seashore, like a musician's thrilled and lifted up by the grand notes of an organ; he may stand wrapt under the mystery of the night sky; find himself touched and moved by whatever is noble, whatever is beautiful, whatever is true, whatever is great in all the world. Such a man as that is a worshipper, and a worshipper of God, if he never saw a church or never read a line of a so-called Sacred Book in his whole life. A man who is thrilled, who is touched by beauty, by truth, by goodness, who is lifted up by the grandeur of the world,— that man, however feebly, falteringly, unconsciously to himself it may be, that man has climbed step by step up the golden, marble stairways of worship that "slope through darkness up to God."

It follows, on the other hand, that there may be very many men scrupulous and particular, who care very much for the mint, the anise, and the cumin, who are very particular about the regularity of prayers, about church attendance, of festivals and of feast days,— who are very scrupulous, I say, in regard to all these things, and who pull their skirts a little closer about them as they pass this other type of man upon the street, lest the infection of his irreligion or infidelity might touch them,— it may, I say, be very well true that this other type of man, called pre-eminently religious, may not have about him one whit of that which is genuine, true religiousness, or worship of the living God. He may care only for these things, while his heart is narrow, while he lives simply for himself, thinks only of his family, the little circle of those whose reflected glory will cast some glory upon him, who only seeks personal advantage, place political or social for himself, who loves to hear men call him Rabbi, who sits in the chief seats in the synagogues,— in the highest places of worship,— and who has not in his soul the capacity to be thrilled with a generous emotion, to be stirred, to be lifted up by anything that is grand and noble. Such a man as this, though he attend church every day in the week, and read the Bible and go through the form of prayer morning and night his whole life through, is irreligious, and is no worshipper of God.

That we then may conceive and understand somewhat the breadth and comprehensiveness of this act of worship, let us look at it for a moment in its threefold character. A large number of the grandest activities of the world have hitherto, on account of the narrowness of our religious definitions, been excluded from any part in the grand chorus of those that have in all ages chanted, "Glory to God in the highest!"

And, in the first place, let us regard the claims of that class of worshippers who almost exclusively, or at any rate pre-eminently, care for the beauty of the world. You will readily see that those I refer to are the ones that we speak of as artists. Are these worshippers of God? and is art a department of divine worship? It has not been so conceived generally. The Puritans in England considered that they were doing God service when they entered the churches and broke down and battered with their sword or their spear everything that appealed to the æsthetic sense, whatever was beautiful. And there are churches still in the world who think that an organ is the invention of the evil one, who have no place for the highest manifestation of music in the service of God. And yet, in the light of the definition of God that we have discovered in this series of sermons, God is the source of the three great divisions of human life. He is the source of beauty, the source of truth, the source of goodness. And these three great departments of human life will, when the world comprehends the breadth and scope of the divine, be included in the one comprehensive act of worship. It is only in modern times that the world has learned to care for the beauty of nature. To be sure, among the old Hebrews and Greeks, and in many ancient nations, that which ever pressed upon them in the grandeur of the sky could not escape their attention. But it is only in the modern world that poets have sung the beauty of nature, that landscape has crept into words and been transferred to canvas,— only in the modern world that this wide realm of the earth beneath our feet and all around us has been thought of as manifesting a spirit of beauty and of life worthy the attention of the greatest minds. The man, then, who, looking out over the world, is stirred by the beauty of nature : the man whose soul is thrilled by the loveliness of the sunrise or the sunset; the man who is touched by the infinity over his head ; the man whose soul is lifted up by the magnificence of the mountains; the man who simply responds to the appeals of the world's beauty,— that man is, so far as he goes, a worshipper, and a worshipper not simply of nature : he is a worshipper of God, who has expressed himself and spoken through the beauty of that world. And he may be religious and a worshipper, so far as this extends, even though he care not one jot or tittle for that which is ordinarily called truth, even though he be unmoral, or even immoral. Take, for example, such a man as Byron as an extreme illustration of what I mean. When Byron describes that magnificent thunder-storm in the Alps,— the finest of its kind that I know of in our literature,— and then goes on and says : —

> "And this is in the night. Most glorious night!
> Thou wert not sent for slumber! let me be
> A sharer in thy fierce and far delight,
> A portion of the tempest and of thee!" —

And when, in contrast to that, dipping his oar at twilight, he sings : —

> "Clear, placid Leman! thy contrasted lake
> With the wild world I dwelt in is a thing
> Which warns me, with its stillness, to forsake
> Earth's troubled waters for a purer spring." —

Or when, looking at the stars that men have aspired toward in all ages, he says : —

> "Whoever looked upon them shining,
> And turned to earth without repining,
> Nor wished for wings to flee away,
> And mix with their eternal ray?" —

Tell me, if you will, that Byron cared nothing for truth, that he cared nothing for the ordinary moralities of life; yet, so far as this magnificent manifestation of God is concerned, that we call beauty, he was a worshipper, and a worshipper of God. So far as it reaches, this is the genuine note of religiousness in the soul of man. And so of the artist who paints pictures, who carves statues, who sings in verse, who pours out his soul in music, who has an ear that, listening, can catch those strange, weird, and mysterious harmonies that sing to his soul while all is silence only to those of duller comprehension. These artists are worshippers; and this is a part, and a very important part, of religion.

And then in regard to that other element, the element of truth, that which is covered by the word "science." Take those men that through their whole lives long, at the cost of self-sacrifice and devotion of the noblest kind, give themselves up to the simple pursuit of truth; who put flattery and honors one side that they may pursue the shadow of truth; who put money one side, as did Agassiz, saying, in some of the grandest words that were ever uttered, that he had "no time to stop to make money," for he had caught a vision of this ideal of truth that flitted before him, and he must follow that. Take the chemist who pursues the mechanism of those marvellous things that we call atoms, dividing them, part from part, until he gets down beyond that which is visible, and then invents all sorts of marvellous instruments that he may take and hold that which the eye cannot see or the hand handle or the ear hear; who pursues it down and down, until he opens at last a little casement that only the imagination can conceive, and through that looks out upon the infinitesimal, the infinitely little, and stands face to face there with God the inconceivable. On the other hand, a man like Newton, who spends his life among the stars, surrounded by the infinitely great; who pursues this search until, in the rapture of his soul, as did old Kepler, he breaks out at last, "O God! I think over again thy thoughts after thee." Or take the geologist, who turns painfully and laboriously, year after year, the leaves of strata that the ages have laid down under our feet; who reads the meaning of the impact and rebound of the little rain-drop that fell upon what was soft sand a hundred thousand years ago; who studies the meaning of the impression of a leaf that belonged to some part of the world's flora long since extinct; who sees and unfolds the significance of a bird-track that belonged to a race that the world has not seen now for many and many a millennium of time. These men that, in any department, at the cost of sacrifice and toil and trouble, devote themselves to unfolding the truth of God, are they not worshippers at the shrine of him who is the God of truth? They may care little for art, for poetry, for music; they may care little for that which technically goes by the name of religion; they may live, like Audubon, for years and years in the woods, never seeing a church or a priest: but they dwell in the very presence and under the shadow of the Almighty.

And, then, that other department, in which alone the world has been accustomed to find true worship,— the worship of goodness, the worship of those men whose sunshiny deeds and words have flashed a rainbow across the age-long shower of falling human tears,— the men who have devoted themselves to helping those who are needy, to alleviating the lot of the prisoner, to struggling for the triumph of the civilization of mankind, those that have been the world's martyrs and heroes, those that have stood forth as the prophets in the dispensation of the highest eras of thought and life, those who have been the great religious leaders of men, whose names have stood even for the one unutterable name of God, — here undoubtedly is that department of human worship which is highest of all. And we are accustomed to lay upon this the grandest, the most significant emphasis, for the reason that here is found the secret of human happiness and human welfare. We can dispense with much that is called science, we can dispense with a great deal more which is called art; but human society cannot exist and human progress is not possible, unless men are true to that which we regard as good, unless they devote themselves to these noble ideals of the moral life of man.

Either one of these three kinds of worship may be followed to the practical exclusion of the rest. Such worship, while true so far as it goes, will thus be distorted and incomplete. Complete worship is the right combination of all.

I want now to raise the question, and answer it briefly as I can, as to whether we are to suppose that God cares anything about our worshipping him. We have seen that God is to be thought of, in our human similitudes and symbols, as conscious, as intelligent, as good. God is our father; and that very word answers it. I believe God does care, that there is a thrill in the infinite heart in answer to this thrill of inspiration and love in our own. Just as every stamp of my foot here on this platform to-day is felt in the sun, however feebly it may be, so the feeblest upspringing of love and adoration in my heart sends out its tiny wavelets clear to the throne of Infinity itself. Here, among men, we do not regard it as an evidence that a man is great and noble, if it be possible for him to outgrow any care for his children or what they may think about him. When a man of towering intellect and genius can stoop to play with the prattling little ones at his feet, to lift them and hold them in his arms, we say that thus he only intensifies and ennobles our conception of that which is greatest in him. Is there any reason why we should think that ignoble up there which we call noblest here below?

Now, then, one practical question: Is it worth while for us to have a day and a place and a ceremonial of worship? I have observed, in regard to all the ten thousand activities of the world, that they are neglected, that they are never done, if they are left at hap-hazard. Men have a time for studying science, if they are interested in it. They have a time to devote themselves to beauty, if they care for it. They have a time to spend with their families, if they love their homes. They have a time to attend to their business. And nothing is attended to in this world, in the long run, that does not have its time. We have inherited this day on which now we are gathered together,— a grand, magnificent opportunity,— and I would devote it to that which represents the largest, deepest, highest interests of man; and I would not allow anything to take away from me the privilege and opportunity of giving at least some part of the day to those things which are highest of all, and which concern the most important part of my being. At the same time, you will readily see how, in accordance with the definition of the meaning of worship that I have given you, it must be proper for us to open public libraries and picture galleries, and make it as easy as possible to empty the weary, worn city into the lap of mother earth, in summer time. I would have this worshipping hour, in which to devote ourselves to that development of life which is called goodness, character, conduct; I would gain from it all the inspiration possible; and then I would make it as easy as possible for men to devote themselves to the other sides of worship that I have spoken of; to look upon images of beauty in picture galleries, to study the truths and the laws of God in public libraries, and to see and smell and hear all that is fair and sweet and restful in the country for those that the town shuts in. And thus this threefold worship of God may find natural and ample room on this one free day.

Now, I want to just give you, in as brief a view as is possible, an outline of my ideal of a place of worship. If we had no house in which we could meet, and it were left to me to dictate as to what it should be, I would have something after the fashion which I will now suggest. I would have a church beautiful in its architecture. I would have one as fine as we could easily and honestly afford. It should stand as the ideal of beauty and of truth. It should suggest aspiration. Its very outline should lead forward and lure upward the thoughts and the emotions. And, then, fine music, as fine as organ tone and human voice could produce. But, the main thing, I would have it fuller of suggestions of the history of the heroism and the glory of man than is Westminster Abbey. I would have it fuller of relic and of picture and of beautiful, suggestive things than any Catholic cathedral of the world. Busts, statues, pictures, relics, and reminiscences of all the grand souls of the world should be in it, so that the eye should light, whichever way it turned, upon some suggestion of human nobility; should see the figure or something to call up the idea of the man who has served his kind in the realm of art, in the realm of science, in the realm of philanthropy, in all departments of life. The great men of our history should be there. The air should be redolent with the perfume of their remembered deeds. The air should be alive and quivering with the whisper of these spiritual presences, and of what they have done for men. And everywhere the soul should see something to suggest the highest possibility of life, something to stimulate and lift up and ennoble man.

And then the internal activities of the church should correspond to all these three departments of worship. It should be a part of our work to cultivate eyes to see and hearts to feel all the infinite forms of the world's beauty. It should not be considered an irreligious thing for us in Sunday-school or on pulpit platform to study and develop scientific truth, to follow and trace the footsteps of God in nature. It should above all be our purpose to make men and women tender and pure, and noble and true. And thus, through this day-by-day and Sunday-by-Sunday worship, we would help lead on the world to the time when, in the words of the grand old *Te Deum*, we should be able to sing, "All the world doth worship thee, the Father everlasting."

SHALL WE PRAY TO GOD?

PERHAPS no subject is more in doubt in the modern mind than this of prayer. On the one hand, there are many who have settled it with themselves that there is no place for prayer in the scientific conception of the universe. If they are in the pulpit, they have dropped this from their public service. Or, in place of it, they have substituted a sort of monologue addressed to nobody,—unless to the audience,—or an apostrophe to the universe in general, with no idea that anybody hears, or that anything is to come of it. If they are in the audience, they wonder why the minister keeps up what, to them, is an unmeaning form, or only a survival of superstition. On the other hand, there are many tender souls who say: "We want to be rational: we admit the leadership of the head; and yet our hearts cry out within us for sympathy and help. We want to pray, and we can hardly help praying." And so, between reason and feeling, they are buffeted this way and that, like a ship in contrary seas, finding no rest. Still a third class is simply bewildered. Not accepting the old ideas of prayer, and not clear in their minds as to whether anything is left, they wait until some deeper thought shall solve for them the problem.

Putting aside all other purposes, then, I wish, in as plain and straightforward a way as possible, to offer what contribution I can toward the settlement of the perplexing questions that involve this theme.

Shall we pray or shall we not pray? This is not, it seems to me, one of the indifferent things that may be done or let alone, and no one be either the better or the worse in either case. If prayer is a means of good to ourselves or others, then we ought to pray. If it is useless, then it is worse than that; for it raises false expectations, leads thought and effort into paths that end nowhere, and is thus a waste of energy that might, in some other direction, be useful. Shall we pray then, or shall we not?

Let us go as near to the root of the matter as we can. When the primitive man first began to pray, what did he suppose himself to be doing? Though bowed before a rough-hewn idol or even a fetich,— stick or stone,— we are not to commit the absurdity of supposing that he was praying to anything that he regarded as unconscious. Our barbaric ancestors had their philosophy or science of things as well as we. It goes without saying, that it was crude and ignorant. But to them, as far as their knowledge reached, it was rational. As their first worship was ancestral, it was to the spirits of these dead ancestors that they offered their first prayers. The dead father or chief of the tribe was supposed to be still alive. He was like them; knew their wants; could sympathize with them; was near, and could hear them. At the same time, as a spirit, he was possessed of supernatural and unlimited resources, and in sky or earth or air, at their request, could produce marvellous and magical results.

But even their crude prayer contained other elements than mere begging. The germ is here of even the highest and noblest blossoms and fragrance that the devotion of the finest souls has produced. They not only asked, but they offered. Not only did they beg for children, for cattle, for success in hunting and fighting, but they also felt awe and adoration and a sense of communion with souls nobler but still like their own.

Which of all these elements that go to make up prayer would be the predominant one would depend on the characteristics of the devotee and on the conception he had formed of his God. I wish you to note this point with special care; for it was not only true of barbaric prayer: it has been true in all ages, and it is just as true to-day. It is said that there is a small tribe in South America whose gods are thought to be so kindly and beneficent that they rarely ask them for anything: they only bring offerings and give thanks. And, if you listen to the prayers of those who think they are civilized, you will notice that some are chiefly begging; others are all thanks; a third devotee is almost wholly wrapt in awe; still another seems all aspiration. And these differences, as I have said, all turn on the personal characteristics of those who pray, and on their conception of the kind of god to whom the prayer is directed. Prayer, in this, is like all other human activities: it will adapt itself, in the long run, to the supposed conditions of success. As a man does not conduct his business in what he knows to be a useless and hopeless way, so neither does he order his prayers in a way that he knows to be useless. If a man asks for rain or health or victory in battle or a good harvest, it is because he believes there is somebody who hears, and who, for the asking, can be prevailed on to grant the request.

Now, this kind of prayer was perfectly consistent to the mind of the primitive man; for his gods were beings of the sky, of the air, of the earth, who, though outside of natural forces, still had some mysterious control over them, and could bring about whatever results they pleased. They were a sort of irresponsible despots. If in some way you could prevail upon them, get their interest or consent, the thing would be done. Substantially, the same idea has prevailed in the popular mind until the present time. The Hebrew Jehovah was a being outside of the natural world, who had created it, and who ruled it as a subject kingdom. Affairs went on after a certain natural fashion, unless he chose for some reason to interfere. But there were ways by which it was supposed he could be induced to bring to pass all sorts of things that, in the natural order of events, would never have happened. The same was supposed to be true of the old pagan deities. If you could get on the right side of Æolus by a present or through the intercession of some other god, he would make his winds blow in the direction in which you wished your ships to sail. If you could gain the favor of Juno or Venus, you could count on their help in a battle. And so, in their sphere, of all the rest. And the matter has not been different in popular Christianity. God has been regarded as a being outside of Nature, has been set over against it, and sometimes almost put in opposition to it. In the popular philosophy, Nature goes on her way, working out certain uniform and unfeeling results; but "prevailing prayer" has a mysterious power over God, and can induce him to bring to pass a thousand results that, but for the asking, would not take place. From the weather and the crops up to the fate of nations and of souls, God is supposed to interfere at the request of men, and to do things he would not else have done. According to the popular phrase I have often heard, "Prayer is the power that moves the arm that moves the world."

What now is the battle between prayer and modern science? Objections of one kind or another against the cruder forms of prayer have been made by the more thoughtful in all ages. But the growth of modern science and philosophy has set the whole question in a new light. Science and the popular ideas of prayer cannot possibly live together. They are mutually exclusive, and one or the other must die. He who believes that modern science is well grounded must reconsider this question. I said, a little while ago, that in all ages prayer had always adapted itself to the prevailing conception of God, and his relation to the universe. The point, then, for us to consider now, is this,— that the growth of modern science has totally changed this conception. Science is not a passing notion of certain eccentric men. It is not something foisted on to the universe. It is simply finding out, so far as it goes, what the nature of the universe is. Now, science has discovered and verified, beyond intelligent question, what has been called "the reign of law." That is, this universe is a cosmos, the scene of an unvarying and universal order. Law is not a something that governs the world: it is only a name for the changeless method by which the power that does govern it works. As science looks at it, God is not a power outside of nature, who can be in some way prevailed on to come in and change it or produce results outside of the natural order. He is this law, this order, in his own personality. Or, to change the phrase, this law, this order of nature, is only another name for his habits of life and work. The throbbing, pulsing life that thrills through all the world is the living God himself, present and working in all. Do you not see the position then? When now I beg of God to modify a natural law, I am asking him to be something else than he already is by the eternal necessity of his being. And this is not true prayer: it is rather impiety.

The popular conception of prayer then, which is a survival of the older and exploded philosophy, is irrational and out of place in our modern knowledge of the world.

Let us look at a few of the reasons that enforce this position.

In the first place, when a man prays that something be done for him, for the mere asking, independently of natural causation, whether he thinks as to what it means or not, he is making the not over-modest request that a miracle be wrought for his own personal behoof. To pray for good health or for a safe voyage at sea or for rain, and so to expect that some power outside of nature will, because of the uttered words, do something that mere knowledge of and obedience to natural laws would not do,—this, I say, is to look for a miracle. To make the matter as clear as possible, let us take for illustration the case of the weather. The condition of the weather over this city of Boston this morning is the last link in a chain of causation that reaches back into infinity. To add to or take away from the atmosphere —except by human agency—one single drop of moisture would be a miracle as stupendous in its significance as the uprooting of Mount Washington and hurling its huge bulk into Portland Harbor.

But man himself can modify the weather and even change the climate of a whole district; and may not God do as much? Certainly, man can modify the weather by a change of the natural conditions, as in cutting down forests or draining marshes; or he may affect atmospheric conditions by a prolonged cannonade. But, in so doing, he only works in accordance with natural law. Mere asking or willing does not produce the results. And, so long as God is thought of as a being separate from the natural laws of the world, of course we can suppose him to act in a similar manner. But our God is not separate from these natural laws. These natural laws are a part of his ways, and they are only a name for his uniform method of working. The cases, then, are not at all parallel.

Is it really a loss to give up the idea that we can change the weather by prayer? We have a Weather Bureau that studies all the natural conditions, and is thus able, with wondrous accuracy, to announce the great changes, the coming of storms and the rapidity and direction of the winds. On our knowledge of these things there depend every week thousands of lives and millions of dollars' worth of property. Suppose now that some unknown man's prayers were constantly liable to upset it all, would it really be a sign of beneficence on the part of God? One of the things I am thankful for every day is that God, even in his apparent severity, is so much kinder to us than our own whims and fancies and follies would ask him to be. Now, precisely this same principle applies to our expectation that, in any direction, God will, for our asking, suspend or interfere with his own natural order.

This leads us to note another absurdity. A large part of this kind of praying is pure selfishness, and goes on the supposition that God is capricious and partial, and may be so worked upon by our petition as to show us a piece of favoritism that, at the same time, will be detrimental to some one else. Suppose I am sailing to Europe, and I pray for favorable winds. Can I prevail on God to forget that somebody else, in as great a hurry as I am, is sailing in just the opposite direction? Or suppose my farm is sandy, and I am anxious for rain: my neighbor's farm may have a clayey soil, and the rain I pray for will spoil half his crops. Whose prayer will he answer out of the infinity of those that are contradictory? Or will he, like a Congressman anxious for re-election, be governed by the wishes of the majority? This latter idea has been gravely argued by certain learned doctors of divinity. Is it not a little better, after all, for us to be able to count on a natural order, and learn, each for ourselves, **to adapt ourselves to the peculiarity of our conditions?**

Then, again, much of our common praying is asking God to put a premium on ignorance and blundering and laziness. Suppose, for instance, I eat and drink all sorts of hurtful things, and then, when I get ill, ask God to make me well again. What am I doing? These laws and conditions of health are God's laws and conditions. Through these, he is every day telling me how to get well and to keep well. And to suppose that I can be well while these laws of health are broken is as absurd as to suppose that a broken organ will produce good music. What would you think of a musician who should take a hammer and pound his piano keys, and then pray to God to make it as good as new again? You would be apt to think a lunatic asylum the proper place for him. But this sort of lunacy underlies the prayer of many a man who thinks it only a proof of piety. Or suppose again I fail to study the nature of the soil on my farm, and so to find out what manures are fitted for it and what crops it will best produce, and then, as the old farmer did, go all over my field and pray in every separate corner that God, outside of natural channels, and to save me the trouble of learning his own ways, will give me a crop such as the natural conditions would not produce? Or, once more, suppose I go to sea in a hulk that is not seaworthy, or in a ship not properly equipped or manned, or that I have not built my ship in accordance with the conditions of fast sailing, and suppose that now I pray that God will let me escape the natural results of my own stupidity? Do you not see that, in all these cases, I am asking God to be what he is not, to do what he ought not, to contradict himself in order to save me the trouble of learning his ways?

Such prayer as this, and a great deal that goes under the name, is simply impiety. Remember, the natural laws and methods of the universe are the present, living God. Here

is the point to keep constantly in mind. If God is perfect,—
and, if he is not, he is not God,— then to ask him to change
is to expect that, to please you, he will become something less
than perfect. It is an assumption on your part that you can
give God valuable advice. As if a fly on the dome of St.
Peter's should suggest an improvement to Michael Angelo!
When Colonel Ingersoll suggested as an improvement to the
universe that "good health should be made catching instead
of disease," he overlooked the somewhat important fact that
good health is catching already. And much of the good
advice that is given to God, in more orthodox quarters, for-
gets quite as important facts. What, for example, can be
more drearily impertinent, to call it nothing worse, than the
staple of ordinary public prayer that gives a weary half-hour
of the congregation's time to telling the Lord in detail all
about the condition of the parish and the affairs of the gov-
ernment and the condition of the world in general, all which
it is to be presumed he knows something about already?
Like the minister Mr. Weiss tells us of, who said, "O Lord,
thou knowest not half the wickedness that is going on in this
town!" Or think for a moment of the scene in Tremont
Temple the other day, when the Rev. Mr. Mallalieu, standing in the presence of the Infinite Majesty, before whom
angels veil their faces, stooped to flinging mud and calling
names concerning a "brother in the Lord" and in the
church, because of an honest difference of opinion on a
matter of practical reform. A squabble of small boys in the
presence of a king on reception-day would have been no
more undignified. And, in all sincerity, I am of opinion that
the drunken drayman on the street, swearing at his horses,
was even less profane.

Or take another phase of ordinary public prayer. It goes
on the assumption that God cares less for his own world and

the souls of his children than the churches do. The constant impression made is that a revival might be started, souls might be saved, the gospel might be carried to the heathen, and so they be saved from hell, if only a sufficient pressure could somehow be brought to bear upon the Almighty. It is assumed all the while that he might, by simply an act of will, do infinitely more than he is doing; but he will not until he is besieged and begged and importuned. What but this is the meaning of the "week of prayer"? If the churches only unite "in a long pull, a strong pull, and a pull altogether," they can somehow get the Almighty started. He sits in heaven and sees souls drop, a ceaseless shower of hissing agony, into hell: he might save them by a breath of his mouth; but he won't, until the churches tire him out with teasing. If God were such as that, I should hold him in contempt. But, since he is not, he must hold the churches in contempt for thinking so. Are men really better than God? Suppose I should go to some loving, tender mother, and beg and plead with her to treat her children decently,— to be kind to them, to clothe them, and look after their little wants. It would mean one of two things: that I intended to insult her; or that I was so nearly a fool as not to know what I was doing. I remember a prayer I used to hear in my boyhood. One phrase, repeated in all prayer-meetings year after year, has burned itself into my memory. A good brother used always to say, "It is time for thee, O Lord, to work!" As though the Omnipotent needed his elbow jogged,— was asleep, or had forgotten about it! If I did not believe God was doing all and the best possible under the circumstances, I would never pray to him again.

And then, once more on this point, there exists no satisfactory evidence that prayer, in this ordinary sense, is ever answered. I am perfectly well aware that whole books have been written full of wondrous answers to prayer, and that it is a frequent topic in the religious papers. But the proof is always about on a level with that which is used to prove that dreams are fulfilled, and that "signs" always come true. There is not one of them that cannot be explained by the ordinary laws of causation. The hits are all remembered, and the misses forgotten.

As a concrete illustration, and one near by, take the case of Dr. Cullis' Consumptives' Home. The good doctor claims, and no doubt thinks, that he cures disease by prayer. The Bible certainly indorses the idea; and no one who believes in its infallibility ever ought to call a doctor. Indeed, the New Testament actually forbids it. It commands any one who is sick to send not for a physician, but for the elders of the church; and not to give medicine or even to regulate diet or look after sanitary matters, but to anoint with oil and pray. I would like to see some consistent Orthodox defend the doctor's calling. It goes right in the face of that which they call the "Word of God." There is a curious condition of things in England to-day. A little sect called the "Peculiar People" attempts to follow this Bible command in cases of disease. And the British nation, calling itself Christian, and holding up the Established Church and the infallible Bible by law, at the same time prosecutes and sends to jail these same people because they obey the Bible. Such is the consistency of those who feel bound to reconcile absurdities.

But to recur to Dr. Cullis. He claims to cure disease by prayer. It is noteworthy, in the first place, that such men only treat chronic diseases where the imagination of the patient plays a large part, and where, under favoring conditions, the recuperative forces of the system may be largely depended on. No one ever tried to set a broken limb by prayer. But even many of these cases die. It is always open, however, to say that the prayer was somehow amiss, had not faith enough, or lacked the right spirit, or else that it was not God's will in that special instance. But, if the person gets well, without much investigation of natural causes, it is all attributed to the prayer. This is about as rational as the trial of witches by the ordeal of water. If they floated, they were guilty and put to death; if not, they were drowned in the trial, and so were got rid of anyway.

Now, it may very well be that a sick man's faith in prayer, and the knowledge that others are in sympathy with him and praying for him, may rouse the energies of his system and send a new thrill of life through his frame. But all this is perfectly natural, and depends on no aid outside of nature. Is it therefore well to cultivate a delusion that is sometimes beneficial? No: for, in many more cases, this looking for help by magic turns away the attention from the real causes of disease and health, and so kills a hundred to one that it cures.

George Müller, in England, has become famous for his hospital, that he claims to support purely by prayer. But it is easy enough to explain the success of such a movement. It needs nothing more than to be known by the great multitudes of sympathetic and generous souls. To be a real test, it ought to be done without any one's knowing it, except him who prays. Miss Mary Carpenter, of London, was one day talking with a person who claimed to be doing a work like this. Said she, "When some person contributes fifty pounds a year toward the support of your institution, do you count that as in answer to your prayers?" "Certainly," she replied. "But," added Miss Carpenter, "in such cases as that, I always put the sums down in my list of annual contributions."

The events, then, that are called answers to prayer, can all be explained in perfectly natural ways; and I, for one, should hate to believe otherwise. One person prays in an agony of soul and with falling tears, and God hears and sends relief. Another cries out of an equal need and sorrow, and the heavens are silent or deaf. Must I think it is whim or caprice? Or may I believe that it is not in this way, after all, that God works? If so, a great burden is lifted off my faith and my heart. Look at the condition of Ireland during the past year. Hundreds starving, and with dry lips crying for food; white-faced mothers looking with anguish on babes whose pinched faces tell of breasts that no longer are fountains of life,— and all for lack of bread. Meantime, heaven is stormed with prayer; and God hears, and answers by miracle. But what is the miracle? Not food, but ghosts of the Virgin and saints haunting old churches, and seen by hysterical women and superstitious priests. Must we accept such a God as that? God answers prayers for deliverance from famine just as soon and as fast as men learn the laws of agriculture, or complete means of communication, by which coming want may be foreseen and provided against.

But, now that this conception of prayer is demolished, is nothing left? Is any one asking: Do you not, then, believe in prayer? And, if you do not, why do you go through the form? My answer is unhesitating and clear: I believe in prayer with my whole heart. And this without any jugglery of words, without any "paltering in a double sense, that keeps the word of promise to the ear and breaks it to the hope."

Prayer is not all asking. Even in its primitive and crudest form, we found it to comprehend awe and adoration and communion and offering. But these things all admit.

It is not around these that difficulties cluster. So I shall pass them by with this word of recognition. Remember that that may be the noblest of all prayer which trusts so completely that it asks for nothing. But as it is about that definition of prayer that confines it chiefly to petition that all the great problems gather; and, as it is my present task to try to solve these problems, I shall confine my discussion to this.

The instinct of prayer, in this sense, is universal. Men have always prayed everywhere. It is a pertinent and important question then for us to ask as to whether this universal instinct is simply a mistake. Does it spring entirely out of ignorance, and will a truer knowledge sweep it all away? If so, we must face it. We do not want to fool ourselves. We shall get on better by knowing things as they are.

But, if this instinct be unfounded, it will be so strange an exception to all others as to make it a greater wonder than if it were true. What is an instinct? Instinct is nothing more nor less than experience become organic and hereditary. It has been created by the nature of things. We stand to the all encompassing God in the universe in substantially the same relation in which a gold coin stands to the die that shapes and stamps it. A universal element of human nature has been created by the reality of things outside of us, and must answer to that reality as the eye answers to the light that made it. To say, then, that this instinct of prayer means nothing and points to nothing, seems to me as irrational as to say that the turning of the compass-needle means nothing, because you cannot find or shut up in a box the magnetic power that turns it toward the poles. Now, then, just what does it mean? We have found that it cannot rationally mean the old and popular notion. What else is left? Let us see if we cannot sink a plummet that will touch hard bottom.

All life hungers. It reaches out, like a flower toward the sun, for that on which to feed and by which it may grow. Man's total nature, from the lowest physical appetite clear up through the mental and moral, until his highest spiritual aspiration exhales like a fragrance toward God, is one grand petition. It hungers; it wants; it reaches out pleading hands toward that which is the fountain of all supply. The body asks, the mind asks. The need for truth, the need for beauty, the need for happiness, the need for good,— all these are so many stretched palms and pleading lips. This is no mere figure of speech. Our total being asks of the universe, the God, about us; and, if we ask aright, the answer comes. This is the root and essence of prayer, whether a word is spoken or not. In the words of the old hymn, supplemented to make it broad enough: —

"Prayer is the soul's"—

or the body's or the mind's, the artistic or the scientific nature's —

"sincere desire,
Uttered or unexpressed;
The motion of a hidden fire
That trembles in the breast."

We are asking God for something every moment of every day, and with every faculty of our being that is alive. Every desire, every effort to get, is a veritable prayer. If we pray with our lips, it is only to give voice to the petition that existed before it was uttered. And the reliance on "much speaking" has been severely condemned by what in the Church at least ought to be ultimate authority; and that on the ground that God "knows what things we have need of before we ask him."

But a large part of our prayers are not answered, while some of them are. What, then, is the condition of a favorable response? The condition is simple, so simple that it is a wonder that people seek it so far away, and do not find it. To make it clear, I must repeat, and ask you carefully to remember what I have already said, that the laws and forces of nature all about us and in us, in the heavens over our heads and in the earth under our feet,— that these are the pulsing, throbbing life and presence of God himself. If we want this God to answer our prayer then, and give us what we need, we must ask or seek in accordance with these laws, on whatever plane of life our desire may happen to be. Suppose we want to raise a cabbage in our garden. Here is the living, present God in soil and sunshine, in rain and dew, telling us to ask aright, and he will answer. But he does not make cabbages grow on stones or drop down out of a blue sky; and he does not make them grow for mere verbal asking. To demand that he shall is to insult him by asking that he abandon his way, and adopt your whim in place of it. But do you say, This is not God giving, but your raising of cabbages? Whose, then, are the soil and air, and sun and rain? With God's part of it left out, how much could you do? Suppose you are in a house somewhere, and are suffering with thirst. You pray for water. A friend suggests that you turn a faucet, and help yourself: does that exclude God as the source of supply? All God's oceans and winds have filled the reservoirs; and the universe, with its everlasting laws, hastens to brim your cup. Some old proverb-maker has said, "The farmer may pray, but he must do it with his hand on the plough-tail." The hand on the plough-tail is prayer in the material realm, and as pertaining to the work of the farmer. It is asking in the only way that will make God hear.

Precisely the same principle holds clear up through from lowest to highest. Knock at nature's door for a scientific truth; knock in accordance with the law of that department in which you are working: listen, and the answer will come. The truth shall be yours. So in the moral realm. Not by mere lip-asking do people become good, but by obedience to the laws of goodness. What else does Jesus mean when he says, "Blessed are they that hunger and thirst after righteousness; for they shall be filled"? In this, the only rational and the only really reverent and pious sense, it is true that "he that asketh receiveth, he that seeketh findeth, and to him that knocketh it shall be opened." In this sense, importunity finds a reason: it is persistence in finding out God's way. But in the common sense, that of pleading with and tiring out God, it is not only nonsense, but impiety.

When we get up into the highest and most ethereal spiritual realms, the same law holds. Spiritual gifts come as the result of our finding out the divine conditions and complying with those conditions.

All prayer, thus, from lowest to highest, so far as we are able to find and obey its law, will infallibly be answered. And not only is this true, but it is also true that nothing ever comes except in this way. Prayer, in the true sense of that word, is the condition of all receiving, in every department of human life. The feeling of desire, the hunger, the reaching out, this is the first step toward all things. So the desire is felt, and the appropriate action follows, it may be a matter of indifference whether it find utterance in words or not. But the prayer must precede the attainment. God will not give anything, bread or goodness, for the mere asking; but, if we ask aright, he will give all we need.

There is time now for only one or two practical words.

And first, if the doctrine I have set forth be the true one, is verbal prayer ruled out? Not at all, it seems to me. The essence of the prayer is, of course, in the emotion, the desire; but the expression of our emotion in appropriate ways is one of the most natural things in the world. We sing when we are happy, we sigh when we are sad. Why not pray when we hunger with unfed longings? And I believe we may properly pray for any and all things, provided — but this is most important — that we only remember that we are thus only pouring out our hearts into the great heart of God; and that this mere asking is not and cannot be a substitute for that which is the essence of prayer. Let us see if this is irrational. I prize my baby's prattle, though it be only prattle. It is my child's life reaching out and up to mine. I am not offended even when a child asks something I cannot give. And, in relation to our child-life toward God, it may very well and very often be that the asking kindles and intensifies the desire that makes the prayer, and that this desire so changes the relation in which we stand to God that channels are opened that had else remained shut, and that through these channels streams of good may flow down that else had not been received.

And, even if the prayer be not answered, it may not be all in vain. I go to a friend and pour out my heart to him, tell him my cares and burdens. He may not be able to touch them with even his little finger; but the thought of sympathy, the escape from the sense of loneliness in sorrow, even this may be unspeakable relief. So, if I take my care to God, and may be permitted to feel that he cares for me, and that the infinite heart thrills with a tender sense of my burden. Though it may not be best that I cease to bear it, and his very love approve my sorrow, still this sense of divine sympathy is unspeakably helpful. Until, then, some one can assure me on unimpeachable authority that God does not feel nor care, I cling to this prayerful instinct that the universe itself is responsible for; and I will still believe that it means what it seems to mean.

But, lastly, what of public prayer? Does that need any defence? A great deal that goes by the name is indefensible. It would be strange if any minister did not sometimes step over the limits of the reasonable. I doubt not I often offend. Jesus condemned the prayer that was intended to be "seen of men." But this does not touch the service of a sincere minister. Instead of praying to be seen or listened to merely, addressing an eloquent prayer to the audience, he seeks rather to be lost in the audience. The ideal prayer is simply a sympathetic voicing of the common aspirations and the common needs. It is not I, it is we. He gathers up and condenses into a cloud the spiritual exhalations of the people, that they may descend again in gentle and refreshing showers.

If then we be men and women of true and tender hearts, if we love our friends, if we aspire toward the things that are above us, if the touch of sympathy binds us to our kind, so that we feel the groaning and travailing of the creation that waits to be delivered, then we cannot help praying in our hearts; and, since the lips are only keys on which the fingers of the emotions play, they will be sure, first or last, to utter themselves in words.

> " For what are men better than sheep or goats,
> That nourish a blind life within the brain,
> If, having hands, they lift them not in prayer,
> Both for themselves and those who call them friends
> For so the whole round earth is every way
> Bound by gold chains about the feet of God."

The Glory and the Shame of Atheism.

THE orthodox Christian tells us that "a dying God" is the necessary condition of human salvation. With a meaning quite other than his, and in a sense far more profound, the saying is true. Only we will put the word in the plural, and say, not only one god, but many, even all the gods of the past and the present, must die in order that man may be saved. The gods have thrived and grown great, have dominated the world and held it in stagnant subjection, because they have fed on human superstition and ignorance and fear. As Apollo was fabled to shoot his arrowy shafts of light through the night-dragons that opposed the coming of day, so the shafts of an ever-brightening intelligence must slay the old-time gods, if a better day is to dawn for the religious life of the world. Only as the gods die is a higher life reborn for man.

Am I then, after all, an atheist in disguise? If what I have now uttered be atheism, I am. Find me any great religious reformer of the past, one whose name stands as marking an epoch in the advance of the world, and I will show you that he was an atheist, as judged by the standards and accusations of his age. It is this atheism of the past that has been the salvation of the world. A history of it is a history of earth's heroes. It is the most significant and hopeful page in the record of humanity. This noble atheism is the glory of the world. As Wordsworth sung of the poets, so would I of the so-called atheists of the past: —

> "Oh! might my name be numbered among theirs,
> Then gladly would I end my mortal days!"

But I am anxious that you should understand me aright. Do I believe in God? I believe in nothing else so much. How, then, can I speak thus about atheism? Listen a moment, and see. Dismiss for a little all thought of what God may be in himself, and ask yourselves what, at any period of the world's history, he must be in relation to the thought of man. In the nature of things, he can be only an ideal; and he may be nothing more than an idol. If only a traditional image,— whether in the mind or out of it,— an idol; if framed of all fresh, living, and advancing thought, still only an ideal. The necessity of this springs out of the fact that God is the infinite, and that man is finite. Being finite, of course we can have only a finite image or thought of that which, on all sides, must transcend all thought. As far as it goes, and for all practical purposes, it may be correct enough; but it must forever fall short of reality. If, then, the human mind and the religious life grow, they must forever be shedding and casting off their old ideals, as the trees drop their last year's leaves. A broader knowledge will slay the old ideal that a new, a higher, and one more nearly approximating reality may take its place.

We sometimes make a difficulty out of this, as though it were peculiar to the question of our knowledge of God. But it is only the eternal condition of all knowledge. We are never sure — if we are wise — that we know anything completely. And, when new knowledge comes, it always brings with it the necessity for a readjustment of our old conceptions

and the formation of a new ideal. For example, we each
have our mental ideals of our friends, of the city in which we
live, of America, of the world. We know that they are all
made of partial knowledge. We do not thence conclude
that these things do not exist, or that it is irrational to study
them. We take the more reasonable course of cherishing
our provisional ideal, while holding it ever ready for change
or enlargement as experience and knowledge increase.

So we have our ideal of God. But the greater part of the
world has not yet learned that it is only an ideal. They confound their mental notion with the reality. And this reality
is to them so sacred that they dare not touch the shadow of
it. The ideal becomes an idol that is blindly and slavishly
worshipped. This idol they identify with God. When, then,
some new prophet of a better day touches this idol, they
attack him with rage and fear,—thinking him really an enemy
of God,—and put him to death. Or, if he succeed in overthrowing the idol, they think religion is dead, and the universe is godless and hopeless. Oh, how many times has this
dreary farce—by the stupid ignorance of religious fanatics
turned into tragedy— been played over in the history of the
world! Let us call up a few illustrations, and thus see who
the atheists of the past have been, and what they have done.
Of course, it is only specimens of the long and illustrious
line that we can notice.

Looming up, huge and indistinct, on the far-off border of
history, where the day fades into twilight, appears the grand
figure of Abraham. And what is that he is doing? In
obedience to what he feels is a higher call, he is leaving
his old home, his father's house, his father's gods, and is
going out, "not knowing whither." O Abraham, we bend
before thee, and hail thee first in the long, historic procession of religious heroes who have made what men call athe-

ism a halo of divine glory! His case presents all the typical features of that kind of atheism that religious contemporaries so bitterly condemn. He turned his back on the old, the established, the traditionally sacred; he left his father's gods; he went out "all adrift," as they say, unsettled, to face doubt, to make a new and "modern" departure, "not knowing whither." To his friends, his people, his old co-religionists, the most sacred thought, convictions, and customs of his time, he was an atheist.

Moses, again, in the eyes of the most magnificent development that the religious life of the race had then achieved, was an atheist. Trained as a priest and prince of Egypt, he denied and turned his back upon all her gods and her religious hopes, and, with a despised rabble of slaves, went out into the wilderness. In after times, it was easy for his followers to say that it was because he sought "a better country"; but, to the most respectable religious opinion of his age, his position was that of a most despicable atheism.

And Buddha, whose name, of all the teachers and leaders of the race, may claim to stand nearest to that of Jesus, — he, too, began his career by an outright and persistent denial of the claims of all the old Hindu gods. He treated them with contempt. Instead of praying to them, he even questioned — so little did they help the world — as to whether they themselves might not stand in need of help.

Zarathustra, the founder of one of the noblest religions the world has ever seen — he, too, was an atheist. Not only did he push the old gods from their thrones, he even made them the demons of his new scheme of the universe; as, in later times, John Wesley is said to have told a Calvinist, "Your god is my devil."

Anaxagoras, the man who hit upon one of the first great discoveries in science, who found out one of God's grand facts, and taught that the sun was a ball of fire,— he, for this, was an atheist in Athens; and, in punishment for his atheism, he was sentenced to death, though, at the intercession of powerful friends, the mercy of a life banishment was granted him. He is only the first in a long line of those who have been declared God's enemies for the crime of discovering God's ways.

Socrates, the noblest man of Ancient Greece, was an atheist, and as such was condemned to the hemlock by his Athenian judges. He dared to believe in better gods than the people could think of or cared to worship.

Jesus was an atheist; and, as they said, a blasphemer, a gluttonous man, a wine-bibber, a keeper of low company, a despiser of the temple, an enemy of all established religion and order. Why? For precisely the same reasons for which to-day he is worshipped as a god. But those who claim, *par excellence*, to be his disciples, seem to learn little of his spirit. In spite of his warnings,— "Your fathers killed the prophets, and ye build their sepulchres"; and again, "A prophet is not without honor save in his own country and in his own house," — they still cling to "tradition" which he despised, and condemn all free thinking which he advocated.

The very name for Christians among the Greeks and Romans was "atheist." And atheists they were. They condemned the gods, refused the popular worship, and opposed all the established religion of the age.

And all down the Christian centuries the same truth appears. Find any man that marks an epoch of religious advance, and you stand face to face with an atheist. Arius and his followers were "devils, antichrists, maniacs, dogs, polytheists, leeches, atheists," in the eyes and on the tongues of Athanasius and his friends. Since Athanasius showed himself such an adept at cursing, it seems peculiarly appropriate that the Athanasian creed, called after his name, should close with a "damnatory clause."

Luther was an atheist in Rome. Servetus and Calvin both were atheists to their opponents.

Giordano Bruno, the first man who in England taught the truth of the Copernican system,— the glory of God, and the commonplace of every school-boy now,—was burnt at the stake as an atheist and an enemy of the Bible. For a similar punishment for a similar crime, Galileo only escaped by a compulsory lie that was called a recantation; though it is said he stamped his foot in anger, and muttered the truth as he rose from his knees. Magellan, too, was an atheist, because he trusted God's shadow of the earth on the face of the moon during an eclipse, and dared thus to assert, contrary to the Church, that the earth was round.

One of the strangest and saddest illustrations of what was called atheism was the case of Vanini, who in 1619 A.D. was condemned to be burnt alive. He declared we could not know God perfectly, unless we were ourselves God. But of Him he said, "He is the greatest good, the first Being, the whole, just, compassionate, blessed, calm; the creator, preserver, moderator, omniscient, omnipotent; the father, king, lord, rewarder, ruler; the beginning, the end, the middle, the eternal. He alone is all in all." And this man, says Prof. Max Müller, was burnt as an atheist. And he was an atheist; for he had denied the popular conception of God, and dared to believe he was better than the people supposed.

Newton, too, was an atheist. When he demonstrated the law of gravitation, the clergy charged him with dethroning God, and putting the universe in the keeping of a law. The same stale charge they are constantly repeating concerning his illustrious successors.

The Church is not yet tired of circulating the falsehoods that became current concerning the famous Frenchman, Voltaire. He is the prince of modern atheists; notwithstanding that he was, perhaps, the first man in modern Europe who built and dedicated a church simply to God. From the Middle Ages down, the churches are St. Peter's or St. Somebody's, until Voltaire, the atheist, inscribes one *Deo erexit Voltaire*,— Voltaire erects this to God. But he was an atheist, for he denied the God of the Church.

In all the pulpits of Christendom and in all her religious papers, Thomas Paine is vilified as an atheist and a denier of future hope for man. Yet he opens his famous book by saying, "I believe in one God; and I hope for happiness beyond this life." His grand creed he summed up by saying, "The world is my country, and to do good is my religion." But atheist he was; and the Church, if she would save herself, was wise to fight him.

We will close our long list with Theodore Parker. The three grand, central, alway repeated words of this great atheist were God, conscience, immortality. Concerning him, Dean Stanley has said that theological science owes to him more than to any man of the century. But the churches have branded infidel and atheist across the forehead of his memory. And thus he takes his place in the long and illustrious line of those who have made atheism glorious.

Who, then, were these men, and what did they do? They were called deniers, negationists, destructives; and the comfortable, the settled, the conservative, have always hated such men, and, I suppose, always will. It is often said of such: "He has told us enough of that he does not believe. I wish now he would tell us what he does believe." So it was said of Jesus. His grand positive assertions of the fatherhood of God, the brotherhood of man, salvation by love and character,—these were all forgotten. It was remembered only that he spoke against Moses and the temple. So now, in spite of the stale charge, that they are always denying, and never asserting, the so-called radicals of to-day are uttering more positive and constructive truth than any other body of men.

Why were these men atheists? For the simple reason that, with a larger love and a larger trust in man and in God, they dared deny the old and popular conceptions in the interest of a broader, grander, and higher truth. Take as a present parallel the attitude of those who deny a literal, fiery hell, and proclaim eternal hope for man. They are deniers. Yes. What do they deny? That God is a fiend, or is impotent. What do they assert? A conception of God so much grander than the old that by comparison the old is a hideous idol. But their very love and faith make them atheists to their time. They see and know that only as the old God is killed off can humanity advance to a higher trust. Yet, of course, those who still believe in the old must regard them as atheistic. To them, they are so.

It may at first seem strange that the very best and noblest men of any age must seem wicked to that age. But the cause is simple enough. The average man must judge his fellows by the conventions and standards of his time. He who loves more than they do, must love some things that they regard as unlovely, and think he ought to hate. He who trusts more than they do, must put faith in things that they think unworthy of it. He must do and say things that they have been accustomed to condemn. Not only was it so with Jesus; but, in any department of thought or life, it must ever be so in the case of him who runs ahead, and so gets out of sympathy with his age. They have no rules large enough to measure him by, and so they pronounce him monstrous. It is so in art and science and morals and philanthropy, as well as in religion.

> "The man is thought a knave or fool,
>   Or bigot plotting crime,
> Who, for the advancement of his kind,
>   Is wiser than his time.
> For him the hemlock shall distill;
>   For him the axe be bared;
> For him the gibbet shall be built;
>   For him the stake prepared.
> Him shall the scorn and wrath of men
>   Pursue with deadly aim;
> And malice, envy, spite, and lies
>   Shall desecrate his name.
> But truth shall conquer at the last;
>   For round and round we run,
> And ever the right comes uppermost,
>   And ever is justice done."

In a similar strain sings Lowell : —

> "Truth forever on the scaffold, Wrong forever on the throne;
> Yet that scaffold sways the future, and behind the dim unknown
> Standeth God within the shadow, keeping watch above his own.

It must always be so, until the world gets wise enough to know that all its best and highest thoughts of God are only provisional, and that the advancing experience and growing knowledge of man is a perpetually unfolding revelation, in the light of which all previous thought must continuously be corrected and readjusted. Who now would set up again on their pedestals the old and moss-grown gods of India, of Persia, of China, of Greece, of Rome, of Britain? Yet, when they fell, their worshippers were confounded, and sent up a cry as though the end of all things had come. Who would rekindle the old altars on which the ashes for centuries have grown cold? Who, again, would listen for the silent voices that once gave divine oracles at Delphi or

Dodona? It was needful that these gods should die in order that man might live a higher life. And, if the world is to see any higher or brighter future, it is just as needful that the popular gods of to-day should also be pushed from their thrones to make way for higher and better ideals. It is impossible that man should become much better than the God he really worships. But the popular ideal of God to-day is not so good as the highest type of man. His thoughts are not so high as our thoughts, nor his ways so loving as our ways. Men are perpetually wishing he was better, and praying to him to be better and kinder than he is. Humanity stands back to the light, looks toward the past, and bends in worship before a crystallized and mummified ideal of barbaric times. No good man would think of defending the God of the popular creeds, if he were found in any other religion than our own. Tradition has sanctified, and made us afraid of him. But he is only an idol. And the real God is away ahead of us, beckoning us on and up along the living ways of his living universe. The only way then to be "a friend of God," like Abraham, — a friend of the living and true God,— is to be an atheist toward the lower and imperfect ideals of the past.

This, then, is the glory of atheism: that, at the cost of contumely and persecution and the scorn of the time, men have dared, and still dare, to listen to the word that came to Moses, and that comes to those who dare to hear in every age, "Speak to the children of Israel, that they go forward!" Thus, it has come to pass that almost all the greatest and best men of history, those whose names stand for new advances, have been cast out by their age. It seems strange that the world does not learn the lesson. As Peschel has said, "The true Creator, because he had acted on the plan pointed out by Copernicus rather than that of Ptolemy, was placed on the Index in the person of those who had made known his system of worlds." And once more to-day, in the person of Darwin, the true Creator is scouted and ridiculed because he did not make the world and man after the fashion that an unknown, barbaric Hebrew laid down for him.

But because this atheism is holy and blessed, and has in it the germ of all future hope for man, is therefore all that goes by the name to be commended? No, by no means. There is an atheism that is hopeless, that is despair, that is death. One face of that which we have thus far treated is true atheism, and should not shun the name; but the other face is the only true and hopeful theism. For, since all attainable conceptions must still be outgrown, if man does not stand still, the old must always die like last year's buds. It is only by thus "forgetting the things that are behind, and reaching forth toward those that are before," that a true and worthy thought and hope of God can be cherished. God is the always pursued, but never completely found.

But, since there is a deadly atheism that is to be feared and shunned, it is needful for us to define it, so that we may be able to distinguish the shame of atheism from its glory? What, then, is an atheist? Let us look at the word. It covers both types, for it means simply a god-denier. Any man, then, who denies another's god, is to him an atheist. But, in the ultimate analysis of it, in modern thought, it means one who denies the existence of any being to which the name God can properly be applied. In that sense, to-day, it is perhaps safe to say there are no intelligent atheists. In the language of the old Psalm, it is only "the fool" who is presumptuous enough to say "there is no God." And even he seems to have been sensible enough to keep it to himself; for he only said it "in his heart"; he did not talk it out among folks. I am aware that the pulpits and religious newspapers are full of talk about "scientific atheism"; and yet there is no circle of recognized scientific men in the world where a positive assertion of real atheism would not be challenged as foolish and unscientific. They would say, No man has a right to deny until he is sure he knows all there is in the universe. So wisely do the religious leaders of the time use words about a science that they do not take the trouble to understand! The most that any man would dare to say would be that he did not know. And some sensible people might be inclined to pardon that as modesty instead of scorning it as impiety. Science is helping to make fashionable what it is to be hoped may yet spread over the religious world,— a modest reticence and humility as to things it does not know.

What, now, is the essence of the idea of God, the denial of which constitutes real atheism? In other words, what must a man deny to be an atheist in the bad sense of that word? It is possible that he may deny the Buddhist god or the Chinese god or the Catholic god, or even your god and my god, and all the time be doing it in the interest of what he regards as a higher and better ideal. But the ultimate reality to which the name "God" really belongs is simply this, — a power outside of us, above us, and about us, by whose laws we are bound, in whose laws is life, in disobedience to whose laws is death. That is, any man who recognizes a law in him, and without him, which binds him under penalty to certain courses of action called right, such a man believes in the essential idea that underlies the word "God." Whatever else he doubts,— whether personality or consciousness or love,— so long as he believes in law, in obligation, in penalty, he believes in God. His God may not be so good, so loving, so hope-inspiring as mine; but still such a man is no atheist.

To the real atheist, the universe does not exist; the cosmos has no meaning. The one, the order, has disappeared. Self is the only law, might makes right, obligation is emptied of meaning,— he is "without God, and" so "without hope in the world." An atheism such as this does really exist; but it is practical, not speculative. It is not formulated in books, for it has no intellectual basis. Perhaps it is safe to say that it is impossible to frame in intelligent language a system of intellectual atheism. The moment the realms of science and law are entered, the facts and laws themselves contradict the theory. But practical atheism is a reality. And, so far as it reaches, it is disastrous in its effects, and deserves all the opprobrium that has ever been cast upon the word. It is a thing of shame, the imputation of which any manly man would resent. I must briefly indicate its features, that we may learn to discern the real enemy of God and man.

In the first place, it manifests itself as an ignorant and thoughtless, or conscious and intended, rebellion against the conditions and laws of life. These conditions and laws are the active, present God. He who allies himself with these laws and forces, gets them behind him, puts himself in accord with them, he becomes strong and mighty. He who opposes them must go under. This holds true whether the laws be in us or out of us, whether we call them material or mental or moral. Opposition to these is opposition to God, and so practical atheism. Whole races, famous men, and men not famous, have tried it, but have inevitably been ground to powder. Rome fell before it; so did Napoleon; so does an ill-constructed house, or the carelessly-made dam of a reservoir. We must learn that we cannot carry our point against, outwit, or "get around" the universe. It is atheism to **do** other than learn and obey.

As this atheism manifests itself in the sphere of morals, it is socially disastrous. Ignoring the law that binds us in duty and obligation to our fellows, we recklessly oppose the God who is "a power that makes for righteousness." Forgetting that duties and obligations are mutual and reciprocal, we obtrude ourselves into the sphere of the rights of others, and find ultimately here, also, that we not only hurt others, but equally destroy ourselves. This is the atheism that recognizes no binding power of right, that makes its own wilfulness dominant, and so seeks to dethrone the force that holds the world in order.

Its ultimate and logical outcome is despair. Seeing no order, no law, no purpose in the drift of things, it comes at last to feel as if the world were like a dismasted and rudderless ship in a storm at sea. It sails toward no harbor, but only drifts, the helpless and hopeless plaything of all aimless, but ultimately destructive forces. It is this state of mind out of which comes crime or suicide, or both. Crime is only a sort of despairing grasp at what one is hopeless of gaining in any orderly or legitimate way ; and suicide is only a giving up of a hopeless struggle with the inevitable.

Real atheism, then, is weakness and despair, a lone battle against the nature of things. Theism is a recognition of the laws and forces of the world, and a conscious union with them in working out some worthy destiny. This is life and strength and eternal hope.

The manly attitude, then, toward the dark problems that surround the being of God, is one of trust and growing faith. This faith and hope are rooted firmly in the experience of the past. They are justified by the experience of man. And, though many times yet the clouds of doubt gather about us, let us not turn back, but boldly face and walk through the cloud. There were no cloud, were there not a sun; and the light is above and on the farther side of the cloud.

"Lo, here is God, and there is God!
  Believe it not, O man!
In such vain sort, to this and that
  The ancient heathen ran.
Though old Religion shake her head,
  And say, in bitter grief,
The day behold, at first foretold,
  Of atheist unbelief,
Take better part, with manlier heart,
  Thine adult spirit can ;
Receive it not, believe it not,
  Believe it not, O man!

"Is there no prophet soul the while
  To dare, sublimely meek,
Within the shroud of blackest cloud
  The Deity to seek?
'Midst atheistic systems dark,
  And darker hearts' despair,
That soul has heard, perchance, His word,
  And on the dusky air
His skirts, as passed He by, to see
  Hath strained on their behalf,
Who, on the plain with dance amain,
  Adore the golden calf.

"Take better part, with manlier heart,
  Thine adult spirit can ;
No God, no Truth? receive it ne'er,
  Believe it ne'er, O man!
But turn not then to seek again
  What first the ill began.
No God, it saith : ah, wait in faith
  God's self-completing plan ;
Receive it not, but leave it not,
  And wait it out, O man!

"Devout, indeed! that priestly creed,
  O man, reject as sin!
The clouded hill attend thou still,
  And him who went within.
He yet shall bring some worthy thing
  For waiting souls to see;
Some sacred word that he hath heard
  Their light and life shall be;
Some lofty part, than which the heart
  Adopt no nobler can,
Thou shalt receive, thou shalt believe,
  And thou shalt do, O man!"

The Intellectual Basis of Faith.*

BY W. H. SAVAGE.

THAT we are living in a new age is a fact seen and confessed by all candid observers. That the systematized conclusions of the past are to be revised, and in important respects modified, cannot well be doubted by any one who has noted the course of events. The seeming adamant of old foundations crumbles in the upheavals of long-imprisoned truth. In the focus of modern light, the old creeds of science and religion suffer

"Change
Into something" dim and "strange";

and the amazed spectators of these transmutations hold their breath, fearing that they themselves, with all their hopes and fears, may presently turn out to be only

"Such stuff
As dreams are made on."

Very momentous questions concerning the nature and destiny of man have been raised, and are to be in some fashion settled, in connection with debated questions in physical science.

These questionings put into a single sentence, and one that utters the intensest feeling of the age, amounts to this:

Are man's religious nature and history correlated to any discoverable and demonstrable facts of a spiritual universe? Or, to put it in other words, *Has man a right to be religious?*

To multitudes, this question, boldly put, has the sound of

---

*A "Phi Beta Kappa" address, delivered at Bowdoin College.

an absurdity. Question as to the divine warrant of religion has never entered their minds. The question, however, has been raised, and must have its answer,— an answer grounded in reason and sustained by adequate witness of facts.

Answer it has had. Very able, learned, and earnest men have given verdict in the negative. Others, also able, learned, and earnest, consent to find place in the future for a sentiment of religion, some vague awe of an unknowable, a dim, dessicated ghost inhabiting the empty space between the tangible world and the abysm of the Infinite.

Neither of these answers appears to be sustained by such testimony of facts as men now demand of theories that come seeking for favorable consideration. The old vindication of religion and the new denial alike fail to meet the demand of the inquirer of to-day.

May we not then hope for attention to a view of the subject that, so far as we are aware, has not heretofore been suggested? There are three ways in which religion may conceivably be justified and established : —

Firstly. On the ground of a supernatural revelation.

Secondly. On the ground of a direct intuition of spiritual facts.

Thirdly. On grounds discovered and established by the method of science.

If the first of these grounds is *real* and *adequate*, we need look no further.

Until quite recently, the reality and adequacy of such infallible supernatural revelation have been affirmed or assumed by the great majority of Protestants. It has been held that the absolute and ultimate facts were given to the world in the Bible, and that the only thing required of man was the acceptance of what was therein given. Inquiry might proceed to the extent of ascertaining the contents of the revelation, but question as to the final authority of these contents was not tolerated.

But the adequacy of this ground for religion is now resolutely questioned. It is seemingly impeached by the fact that other grounds have been and now are sought for by writers of religious apologetics. The very remarkable "Monday Lectureship" takes its stand openly on what it calls science, and claims the suffrages of believers on the basis, among other things, of the announcement that it knows of a microscope that "begins to have visions of immortality." The *possibility* of supernatural revelation being granted, debate still rages about the question whether the *possible* has ever emerged into the *actual;* and there are no signs of such a settlement as will give much solace or assurance to earnest minds. It is enough for our purpose to know that the anthropomorphic and miraculous religion of tradition has ceased to control and satisfy the minds which are giving direction to the inquiries of the modern world.

We may therefore proceed to inquire how things stand with the second method of coming at the facts that underlie and authenticate religion.

This may be sufficiently described by calling it the method of *intuition*.

Coleridge, if not the founder of this method, may be said to be its most conspicuous representative in its modern form. The ground of religious obligation and hope is found by him in truth immediately, and in some ineffable way, *seen*. "Faith" to use his own words, "consists in the synthesis of the reason and the individual will. . . . By virtue of the former (that is, reason), faith must be a light, a form of knowing, a beholding of truth."

This, as I understand it, is in substance the doctrine of the modern members of the intuitional school. Says a recent very able writer, "My *intuition* is my *looking upon reality*."

One of the first things that strikes us in glancing over the history of the Transcendental Philosophy is the fact that the results of the alleged direct vision of truth furnish a constantly narrowing foundation for a theological superstructure. At first there was room, according to Morell, "to ground the great doctrines of Christianity upon a philosophical basis without . . . detracting aught from their peculiarly evangelical characters"; but now the habitable area of the flying island, that after its eccentric voyaging seems about to dissolve into the mist from which it was compacted, scarcely suffices to sustain two or three half-finished columns of that imposing temple that was to shelter the human race. The religious bodies, that at one time seriously meditated the removal of their seminaries to this New World, have decided to remain where they were. If ever the shade of Coleridge revisits the scenes of his former theologizings, the men he meets are by no means distinguished for their zeal in church-building. They are known rather for their success in exterminating the unfortunate pioneers of the old faiths, who had come to spy out the land; and now, having everything their own way, and feeling lonesome, they are seemingly looking for more worlds to conquer.

The effort of Coleridge to find in the philosophy of Kant the means of making this philosophy deny its maker must, I think, be regarded as a failure. Allowing what I do not allow, that there is warrant in Kant's doctrine of the categories of thought for the statement that there are "certain primal ideas and sentiments given in the constitution of the human mind," Kant holds that these ideas can have only a subjective validity, and that reasonings which assume the **existence** of corresponding objective realities of being **are** pure illusions. The reality of the soul, of the universe, of God, could, he held, by no process of the pure reason ever be established. To every argument adduced to prove objective reality, he was ready to respond with unanswerable objection. Subsequent explorers following in the lines of his speculations have, so far as I know, added nothing to the known or the knowable by means of the transcendental philosophy. Its total result is given in the Tennysonian maxim, "We have but faith: we cannot know"; and the final consolation of religion from this source is the rather unsatisfying reflection that, if she cannot demonstrate her right to live, nobody can prove that it is her duty to die. If this is the final word, there needs no special inspiration to foretell the event. In an age that had not seriously questioned the reality and infallibility of revelation, that had fixed religious habits and traditions and a large accumulated capital of reverence, religion could maintain her ancient prescriptive rights. But the world is becoming somewhat crowded now. The veteran that "lags superfluous on the stage" finds small reverence. There is a visible weariness and impatience with institutions that merely apologize or challenge the world to produce the official text of the divine decree that orders them to vacate the premises. The Church's asseveration, that according to its best knowledge and belief there is the material for a rational and binding creed, if it could only find out where this material is, and then find out how to get it, will not avail as a final answer for those who see no real steps taken in the direction of either of these discoveries. We are in a world in whose struggle for "survival" the "fittest" is that which can show the best visible reason for continuing to be.

We come now to the third on the list of possible grounds for religion,—discovery of truth by the scientific method.

Man has been defined to be "a religious animal"; and he has justified the definition in both its members,—the "animal" as well as the "religious."

We are informed by exponents of the more recent science that this definition was framed by man to fit a condition which had back of it an indefinite immensity of time, during which there was proceeding a growth toward the stage of self-conscious life, in which man could reflect on himself and give himself a name. Time was in this immensity when the "animal" was "religious," after a fashion very unlike the present. Back of that a time when there was simply an "animal" with "religious" possibilities, like the possibility of eyes in a creature merely *sensitive* to light, but with no developed organs of vision. This possibility has become now an organic fact. The religious factor in man has become the controlling element in the history of society. It has inspired oracles, organized institutions, created literatures, builded and destroyed civilizations. What was once held to be a Heaven-descended revelation is now said to be the product of the human mind. Man has himself created the thing he afterward attributed to his God, and in a sense the God to whom he attributed it. There is that in him that thinks things so divine that he has believed himself to have vision of the invisible God. The question that waits to be answered is this: How shall these facts of human nature and experience be accounted for? The supposed supernatural revelation, the intuitional philosophy, did not, we are assured, create the things they sought to explain, but were themselves the creations of that for which they tried to account.

My speech has already "bewrayed" me as an evolutionist. I frankly confess myself a believer in the essential doctrines of Darwinism. Let it be understood, however, that my aim is not to establish the evolutionary hypothesis or to justify the evolutionary philosophy. I *accept* these for the time being; and my aim will be to show that, being taken for granted, they furnish a firm ground for the superstructure of religion.

Several times already in the history of the world, religion and society have found their saviors in those who were anathematized when they appeared, as the foes of both. Quite possibly, "the thing that has been is the thing that shall be" again. At present, it seems quite evident that religion must live, if she lives at all, in a world that accepts the doctrines of evolution. It is plain, moreover, that, living in the same world, they must agree.

Now, if religion is grounded in the facts of the world, there is the best of reasons for believing that essential and permanent religious facts will find their natural and most fitting expression in the language that gives expression most naturally and most adequately to the other related facts of the world; for this universe is all of a piece, a kosmos. The clew that leads us in the real track of the divine order in the lowest ranges of being will, if held and followed, conduct us to the highest revealings of the universal life.

Suppose, then, that we try the ascent from the plane of physical facts to the facts of man's spiritual experience, holding in our hands the clew of evolution.

Our first task is to learn whether the accepted facts of religious experience will bear translation into the language of evolution, without suffering violence in the process. Not long since, a gentleman, in criticism of some of these ideas, remarked that they "translated accepted facts into the language of evolution, without giving to them any additional validity."

Now let it be remarked here in advance that the scientific

adherents to the hypothesis of evolution do not claim that their doctrines offer an exhaustive explanation of anything. Evolution stands as an *hypothesis*, and furnishes a *method*. Without attempting to answer the question of *origin*, it offers a solution of the subsequent question, How came the present out of the past? Its answer is: The world was not *made* by a kosmical carpenter. It has *grown* by natural and vital processes. This answer *unifies* the entire physical history of the planet. One fact grasped and understood furnishes the key to the whole immense order. Facts repugnant to all other hypotheses come into harmony under this; law and order extend daily their joint empire over the ancient chaos.

A vast gain has then been made when "the accepted facts" have been "translated into the language of evolution." No "additional validity" has been given to these facts, and they need none. *Facts* can go alone. It is the *theory* that asks for "additional validity." And this "additional validity" it gains, when the facts ask to be translated into its language.

Now, if religious facts will bear translation "into the language of evolution," if they suffer no violence in such treatment, if, on the other hand, they fall into orderly relation and natural sequence, we are justified, I submit, in holding: —

1. That these facts are a part of the natural order of the world, and so reveal the working of a power in Nature which is distinctively related to the religious faculty in man.

2. That we have found the true method by which to prosecute farther inquiry into the meaning of these facts.

3. That we are justified in expecting to have some time a *science* of religion.

4. That this science will harmonize with and supplement physical science.

5. That religion will stand with a demonstrated, divinely natural right to the highest place among the shaping forces of the world.

These, it strikes me, are substantial gains, not to be despised, at any rate until there is something considerably better than the present chaotic and demoralized condition of religious thought.

Now for the attempt at translation.

"The hypothesis of evolution," to quote Dr. Draper, "asserts that from one or a few original organisms all those that we see have been derived by a process of evolving or development. It will not admit that there has been any intervention of divine power." *Assuming* the original organisms, evolution teaches us that these originals possessed a tendency to develop in lines of resemblance to the primal type, and that there was also present a tendency to develop such modifications of this type as would bring an organism into harmony with the world about it,— that is, its "environment."

So much having been postulated at the outset, science tells us that the forms of organic life, at any and every point in the world's history, have been shaped by the physical surroundings. The development of a plant is determined, among other things, by the climatic conditions under which it grows. The plant of the Tropic is unlike that of the Arctic Circle, because the "environment" has made it so. The feet of the modern horse are unlike those of his remote ancestor, because the conditions of his life are unlike those amid which the four-toed orohippus lived. The teeth of various creatures reveal the food conditions which surrounded them. The lungs give us the quality of the atmosphere furnished for breathing. So universal and so exact has been and is this correspondence between the organism and its environment that it has been held to furnish the most convincing proof of the work of a designing mind in the ordering of the world. "See," it was said, "the wisdom and the goodness of God in adapting the world to the wants of living creatures." A whole literature of religious apologetics sets forth this demonstration of natural theology, and college professors enforce it upon their classes to this day.

The new science, however, teaches that this correspondence between organism and environment is the work of the environment itself. As conditions have changed from age to age, organic life has been subjected to the compulsions of new surroundings. What the environment could not reshape it destroyed. The plants and animals that survived the great changes of the past were those that were able to endure such modification as would set them in harmony with the new order of things. This is why there were so few facts to mar the demonstrations of Dr. Paley and his school. "Dead men tell no tales."

Man, like all his humbler relatives and neighbors, is included in the scope of these statements. As an animal, *he is the resultant of his environment.* Granting heredity and adaptation, the environment must explain the *special* result. It is *this*, and not something different, because the environment has been what it has been, and not otherwise. In other words, certain objective forces operating through vast periods of time have determined man to be what we see him to be at present.

To illustrate: Man's lungs are what they are as the result of the atmosphere in which they have been developed. Restore to the atmosphere the carbonic acid eliminated during the formation of the coal measures, and **man** would at once perish. The Saurian successor of Dr. Paley would construct the demonstrations of his natural theology **undisturbed** by any human protest.

Man's ear is the creation of the vibrations that convey sounds. Had there been no vibrations, there would have been no ear. Should these vibrations now cease, the ear would in time disappear from the organism. Renew them, and they would recreate the organ that should perceive them.

The eye is the creation of the light which it now sees. Had there been no light, there would have been no eye. Shut a race of men in a sunless cavern and enable them to exist, and there would be seen a retrogression toward the brute, resulting in time in deformed and eyeless remainders of humanity.

In a word, for every fact in the physical constitution of man, as we see him to-day, there is a corresponding creative fact or force in the environment, which has been for countless ages operating upon him, and making him what he is.

An orderly, classified, and duly correlated statement of these facts, so far as they are known, we call physical science. Physical science is, therefore, *what men know* about those realities, those forms of the universe that *touch* and *shape* man's physical nature. Men know nothing and *can* know nothing of what does not touch them. In other words, science originates in *sensation*. "Nothing in the mind which was not first in the senses," said John Locke. "Except mind itself," added Leibnitz. And for a time it seemed that Leibnitz had pointed out a defect in the Lockian philosophy.

There was a time, however, when the facts of nature, as real and as actively operative as now, were entirely unknown to the primeval man, who had been in a very important sense created by them. The stuff of the future science, and, so far as we can see, of the mind that was to construct it, was as yet in the *senses*. The future philosopher was simply a creature who *felt* the environment that was creating him.

Then, as time went on, conscious mind began to look from the eyes that surveyed the scene of nature. Man, who had before *felt*, now *knew* that he felt. Then arose questionings as to the origin and meaning of his various sensations; and man began, in a dim, tentative way, to study nature, trying to find out the objective fact that gave rise to his subjective experience. In other words, he entered upon a course of discovery according to the scientific method. Having learned by experience to postulate an external cause for a large number of his sensations, he sought to make the passage from his inner experience to a knowledge of this external world in which the causes of his sensations were located.

An oyster lying in the shallow, sunny water *felt* the light, but knew not that he felt it, and knew not that it came from the glowing disk in the sky. Hence there is as yet no oyster theory on the subject of light,—*none that I know of.* But a man, sitting once on a sunny bank, felt the same vibrations that reached the oyster. *He* said, "*I* feel the light." He isolated himself from the world about him. He said, "This is I: that is the sun." Starting from a single ascertained fact, he felt his uncertain and stumbling way across the threshold of knowledge; and there, in the vestibule of history, science was born, a bantling, weak and dim-eyed as the man who nursed it, but incarnating "the promise and potency" of the differential calculus and the *Mécanique Céleste.* Up the dim track of æonian time, the man and his attendant spirit have come together. Now worshipping it as a god, now fearing it as a devil, now consulting it for oracles, now exorcising it "as 'twere the fiend," man has dared neither to forsake nor to follow the shape that in ghostly guise has seemed now his shadow and now his guide. Only yesterday, as it were, did man awake to the fact of his kinship with the world about him. *Now* he sees in it his physical creator, his muse, his teacher. The dead world lives. Evolution has not exhausted its mystery. Every molecule is a window that opens on a prospect toward the Infinite. But at last man has an introduction to his Maker, and walks in his thoughts in the tracks of the Almighty.

This, then, is the story of physical science.

1. Man's physical nature has been made to be what it is, *rather than something different*, by his environment.

2. Man, having risen to the possibility of conscious sensation, *felt* his environment, which still continues to press upon him.

3. Man began to employ his thinking faculties, and by a process of discovery according to the scientific method made the passage from sensation to knowledge of the objective facts.

Now, I venture to advance the opinion that the religious history of mankind has followed a line precisely parallel to this story of physical science.

In other words, I hold that there is sufficient reason for believing that man's religious nature has developed under the controlling and shaping influence of an environment of spiritual facts or forces; that, corresponding to each of the great, constant facts in this religious nature, there is a creative fact or force in the environment; that but for these objective realities, acting upon him and creating him, no such "*religious* animal" as man has been and still is would have been possible.

I hold that all real gains in religious knowledge, all advances beyond the *spiritual sensation* produced in man by his environment of spiritual facts or forces, have been made by discovery and verification according to the scientific method.

And, further, it seems to me capable of proof that the

knowledge that men claim that they gain by "faith" or by "the heart" is in fact simply hypothesis which they make to account for certain real or supposed spiritual experiences. In framing such hypotheses, men stand upon the vantage-ground of inherited aptitudes and acquired knowledge, or upon the disadvantage-ground of inherited misconception and acquired ignorance. In either case, an application of proper critical tests never fails, I think, to show that "faith" and "the heart" furnish *hypothesis* as distinct from *knowledge*.

To set our theory of man's religious history in terms that run parallel with the account that science gives of his physical history, it appears: —

1. That man's religious nature has come into existence as the correlate of certain creative spiritual realities, and that it has been made to be what it is, rather than something different, by the facts of environment.

2. That when man had arrived, in his development, at the possibility of a religious consciousness, the pressure of his environment awoke in him the spiritual faculty that responded to its suggestions.

3. That man then began to employ his thinking powers upon the matter of his experiences, and by a process of discovery according to the scientific method slowly made the passage from what we may call spiritual sensation to whatever knowledge he now has regarding the objective facts.

Now let us give our reasons for holding these articles of belief.

To begin with the first: —

There are two possible hypotheses which may be advanced, in harmony with the doctrine of evolution, to explain the facts of man's religious history.

First, we may suppose that the original organism from which man has developed was, by a designing mind, so framed that it *must*, under the conditions that were ordained for it, produce the actual facts of the world's religious history.

Granting the correctness of this hypothesis, we have an explanation of history and a firm ground for religious obligation and hope. We have also a confirmation of my position that for every essential fact in man's religious nature we have a corresponding creative fact or force in his environment.

The second possible hypothesis is this: We may suppose that the initial point of human history was the arrival somehow upon our planet of a germ with simply the capability of developing under the influence of its environment and in harmony with it. In that case, the *development* will reveal *the nature of the forces that act upon it.* Any well-defined and essential trait in the religious nature of man will then necessitate belief in a reality of environment correspondent to it and adequate to produce it; for, by the terms of the hypothesis, the germ was simply a plastic possibility. It contained no element of compulsion toward either *direction* or *result.* The only possible explanation of direction and result must then be found in spiritual forces directing and shaping it.

Let me illustrate my point.

In waters reached by the sunlight, we find fish with eyes. In Mammoth Cave, we find fish without eyes. In the germ from which fish came there was, then, no *necessity* compelling the formation of eyes. There was in it the *possibility* of eyes. The *necessity* came in the sun-ray. That turned the *latent possibility* into an *organic fact.* Without that coming, the possibility would have remained unrealized; or the coming of some other force *might* have developed this latent capability of vision into some other entirely different manifestation. We know, at any rate, so much as this: that eyes do not appear except as correlated to the objective fact of light.

Now, I think there will be small dissent from the statement that man's religious nature is as much a distinct *fact* as his eye or his ear; a fact, too, not to be confounded with its accidents. The products of this nature are as real and as unescapable as any building of pyramid or mountain. The essential elements in the ideas of God, duty, truth, right, immortality, seem as much matters of course in the order of nature as the secretions of bodily organs or the deposition of rock strata.

These things being so, they require to be accounted for. No scientific account of the world can be complete that does not account for these ideas, and their influence in history, fairly and adequately.

Now, it is simply scientifically inconceivable that man should have become what he is, unless these results of history were either foreordained in the germ — in which case, essential Theism with its logical accompaniments is granted — or produced by a spiritual environment, involving at least as much as we mean by Theism.

That from a simple cell, without predetermined necessity of growth and left simply to the influence of surroundings, there should have come forth the actual history of humanity and the thoughts "that wander through eternity," while in the surroundings there were no realities correspondent to the visible results, — this were a thing to overturn the very axioms of science, and make reasoning henceforth impossible. The obsolete church dogma of creation out of nothing is "milk for babes," beside such a stupendous contradiction of reason as this. If the hypothesis of evolution holds good in physics, it must also hold good in religion. On purely scientific grounds, the religious nature in man demands a reason in environment just as imperatively as the eye or the ear. Man has, as simple matter of fact, if his history has been such as evolution declares it has been, been lifted from the levels of the tiger and the ape. He has written the prophecies of Isaiah and the words of Jesus. He dreams of things that no pen has been able to write, and no speech can translate into the stamped currency of religion or philosophy. The dullest churl may sometimes be seen turning dim eyes, that seem at once blinded and fascinated, toward the same ranges of infinity that prophet and poet have scanned with rapt faces "as they watch for the morning."

I can find no solution of all this that seems at all adequate, save that which Tennyson has put in form, as exactly scientific as it is beautiful: —

> "Out of darkness came the hands
> That reach through Nature, moulding men."

Man is a result. He has been *made*, somehow, *all of him*. He cannot transcend his cause. The force that has shaped the highest in him may be harder to find than that which shapes his physical growth, yet none the less it must exist.

My second proposition was that man was at first simply *sensitive* to the spiritual facts amid which his self-conscious life began, and that the religious faculty in him was aroused by the touch of the spiritual environment.

The evidence for this may be said to be the religious history of mankind.

There is no semblance of evidence for any such primeval revelation as men have imagined for theological purposes; and the notion is now given up in intelligent circles. As little reason is there for believing in the fancy that the primitive man had any intuitional knowledge on religious subjects. All that we see is a dim religious *feeling*,— an awe of the Unknown,— which may, I think, be most fitly described as the beginning of *spiritual sensation;* a *feeling* of the environment that, operating upon a responsive nature, awoke in man the beginnings of the religious sentiment. It was the spiritual analogue of man's first recognition of the external world as something other than himself, with power to produce sensations in him.

I should not say it was "the heart" that felt this, though I do think that what is sometimes called "heart-religion" is, when it is not a fraud, the modern form of this original spiritual *sensation*. People still *feel* the unseen; and the "faith" that is good, and ought to abide, is the confidence that this *feeling* is valid evidence of an objective spiritual reality. But we should be careful to remember that neither the *feeling* nor the *faith* can be trusted in the manufacture of religious dogmas. *What* it is that touches us, that we feel, in the reality of which we "have" and ought to have "faith," is a matter to be settled by the tests of reason, when the grounds of judgment are sufficiently explored.

That man's first response to the touch of the spiritual environment was strictly analogous to his response to the touch of the physical world is, so far as we can now see, historic fact. He recognized simply *power*, which might help or harm him; and he adopted such a course of action regarding this power as his very limited knowledge suggested. He fancied it resident in certain mysterious objects or in certain unexplored places. He bargained with it for exemption from the harm it might inflict or for the good it might bestow. Light and darkness were not yet divided. Nature and God were but phases of an unknown universe. He knew simply that there was an external something that he could not escape from, a something that beset him on every side, and incessantly challenged inquiry and explanation.

That man has endeavored to make the passage from *sensation* to *knowledge* is only too well known to all students of scientific and religious thought. How this attempt began in physical matters, and in what it has resulted, is recorded for all readers in the history of science. How it began and how it has proceeded in religious matters will be more clearly seen, when men have so conquered their prejudices as to be in condition to listen to the witness of facts. It is beginning to be seen already, and what is seen is in perfect harmony with the doctrine I have thus far advanced.

Man gave something like three thousand years to making and trying assumptions in physics. In this way, most of the follies and impossibilities were tested and exploded.

Just so it has been in religion; though in this field progress has been hindered by the fact that an exploded folly has pleased the mass of men about as well as an unexploded one, and rather better than a solid fact. But, in spite of this, a rude and tedious application of the scientific method has been clearing the field for the new age, in which a religious science shall explore for truth. Much valuable material has been accumulated in observed and classified facts concerning man and nature; and, looking along the lines of advance indicated in the results of a scientific study of man and the world, the conclusion seems to me no longer doubtful.

How we are to make the passage from the facts of physical science to the *power* which science *reveals*, but cannot *see*, is a problem yet unsolved. The solution, we are told, is inconceivable. Let us, however, remember the saying of Goethe,—"Man must persist in believing that the inconceivable is conceivable, or he will never make a discoverer."

One thing is settled. The universe is not a pretence, with nothing in it or above it. Herbert Spencer has made an atheistic philosophy impossible. *We* may not be able to apprehend his "unknown"; but what *we* cannot grasp, men of completer growth may be able to reach. Evolution, with its doctrine of growth, puts a logical quietus on dogmatism about the limits of discovery.

How we shall make passage from man's nature and history to a knowledge of the spiritual powers that have been and are creating him, no one may be able now to say. But no man is authorized by any scientific fact or law to say that the passage cannot be made. To the objection contained in the statement that we cannot deal with what lies beyond our experience, it is sufficient to say that all growth comes into contact with what was beyond the former experience.

Meantime, it is something surely to have valid, scientific reason for holding to the substantial, creative verity of the spiritual forces that stand correlated to the spiritual nature and experience of mankind; to have a religious method that unifies the world's history and prophesies of a day when science shall be religious, and when religion shall be scientific.

It remains for me to indicate briefly the bearing of this subject upon the question of method in religious inquiry.

I have asserted that "faith" and "the heart," using these words in the sense commonly given them in religious circles, furnish *hypothesis* as distinct from *knowledge.*

Tennyson grants this unreservedly, as we have seen. "We cannot know," is his conclusion. His "faith" is simply an hypothesis which he confesses himself unable to verify.

But this conclusion of the great poet is by no means the favorite one in ordinary religious circles. Things visible and invisible, things impossible and things inconceivable, are there *known* "by faith"; and very frequently men's "hearts" tell them things that no sanely intelligent man would care to be held responsible for in a court of justice, or in the court of history; and all this without the troublesome processes of inquiry and verification.

But even these foolish and harmful excesses of religion bear most impressive though indirect witness to the truth of my positions.

That there should be a very persistent and controlling religious belief among men who know nothing about the scientific method, or any other method of thinking or investigation, is precisely what we should expect, if the doctrines I have advanced are correct. Human nature, having been made what it is by the environing realities with which religion has to do, should of course be responsive toward those realities. Among men of untrained minds, hypothesis and assumption stand as substitutes for knowledge on all the more mysterious questions. This is specially true in religion. All men can *feel* here; but only a few are capable of subjecting feeling to a critical analysis, and finding the fact revealed in it. The common element in human experience is the belief in an objective ground of spiritual sensation. This belief has become, in a sort, a second nature. The form under which the individual conceives these unseen powers to exist and act upon him is determined by the general thought of his age. Belief abides because of inherited habit and personal experience. Tennyson has put the common form of religious demonstration in his verse:—

> "If e'er, when faith had fallen asleep,
>   I heard a voice, 'Believe no more,'
> And heard an ever-breaking shore
>   That tumbled in the Godless deep;

> "A warmth within the breast would melt
>   The freezing reason's colder part,
> And like a man in wrath the heart
>   Stood up and answered, '*I have felt.*'"

The fact that this is the answer of mankind as a whole to the voice that says, "Believe no more," bears eloquent witness to the divine elements in the working forces of the universe; but that is a fatally defective philosophy of human life that has no other answer than this to give, when put to the question by the modern *Zeit-Geist*. If this is all, then religion not only *begins* in feeling, but there *ends*. The liberty to indulge in a decorous emotion when the feeling is stronger than usual is all that she can ask or receive. By no possibility can any firm ground of reason be found in the chaos of "worlds unrealized." By no divine astronomy can the fixed lights of truth be distinguished from the tapers that glimmer in fogs of tradition that overhang the labyrinthine ways of metaphysical theology, or from the *ignes fatui* that lure the multitude into the bottomless bogs of superstition. Religion must take refuge in the cell of the monkish traditioner, in the ecstasy of the mystic, or sit with the rapt poet, far from the common life of men, above the clouds that shut its turmoil from the sight of heaven.

Here and there, one abiding in the lofty calm of contemplation may say to the questions that follow to vex him,—

> Here "in my spirit I will dwell,
> And dream my dream, and hold it true."

But, in the great world of action, ignorant enthusiasm will shame religion by its excesses, and culture will leave "faith" to fools.

The verse of Tennyson, like much religious philosophizing, illustrates the too common tendency to give a very inadequate reason for most excellent behavior. There are far better grounds than he alleges for refusing to be an atheist. The man Tennyson himself stands as an adequate and unanswerable scientific rejoinder to the sceptic Tennyson's "freezing reason." Science, taking his own "In Memoriam" and planting itself on the ground of Darwinism, may safely abide the severest tests of fair investigation. That poem is as real as the solar system. Its religious aspiration, longing, and faith must have a ground in facts of the universe. As well believe the great star Alcyone to be but a fancy born of some cheating trick of the optic nerve as believe that a starlike thought, shining in the infinite empyrean of the soul, is but the glint of two clashing atoms in the brain of a man who does not know enough to locate the flash, as he should, in the gray matter of the cerebrum.

But if the poem refutes the carpenter-philosophy of the system-builders who potter in attempts to construct a universe that shall stand firmly on nothing, if it defies the chemistry of experimenters who think to extract sunbeams from fungus growths that never saw the light, what shall we say of the poet himself?

The grandest glow of poesy that ever belted the spiritual heavens with its galaxy of "words that burn" is less wonderful than is many a soul that walks the common round of duty here on the earth. Whence these spirits that enshrine the awful beauty that enthrones itself in the worship of the ages, spirits from whose altitudes one looks with almost level eye upon the fixed lights of Eternal Truth? Not accidents: there are no accidents. Not freaks of nature, fountains that leap above their source. Science knows nothing of things like these. And, unless science is one stupendous mistake, and its doctrine of evolution a denial of Cause, we are brought into the presence of environing realities, so transcendent that the intellect in its loftiest mood must stand abashed before the majesty

> "Of Something felt, like something here,
> Of Something done, it knows not where,
> Such as no language can declare."

Taking these facts of man's nature and history, let Religion quit her abject attitude of apology and her futile iteration of creeds outworn. Let her come fearlessly forth from the cell of a "faith" that cannot "know." Her facts are as real as the facts of geology. Her fear to trust them and build upon them raises the suspicion that her "faith" has damaged its eyes by long musing in the dark, or that she cares more for the safety of catechisms than for the real truth. By adopting the method of science, she may rid herself of the impediments of error, attest the enduring validity of the divine elements of her experience, and open the way to grounding her hopes on discovered and demonstrated reality.

By such a course, Religion will take her rightful place as queen of the sciences. She will have a method, and be able to make good her claim. She will stand hopefully fronting the future, her feet planted on the solid facts of the universe. She will have left to her all that is worth preserving from the things that have been supposed to rest on grounds of supernatural revelation or of intuition; and will have besides the very great comfort of being able to give a reason for continuing to believe them. Reason and reverence will stand together at her altars; and to the litany of their worship all the people will say, "Amen!"

"*A VERITABLE HAND-BOOK OF NOBLE LIVING.*"

THE DUTIES OF WOMEN.

A COURSE OF LECTURES

By FRANCES POWER COBBE.

CRITICAL NOTICES.

An eminent American clergyman, writing from London, says: —

"It is the profoundest, wisest, purest, noblest book, in principle, aim, and tone, yet written upon the True Position of Woman in Society. It should be circulated far and wide among all classes of our countrywomen. It should be made a class-book in our schools. It should become the 'Hand-Book' and *Vade Mecum* of young American girls."

"As I turn the pages of this book, I am struck with its candor, sympathy, and insight, and wish that it might be read and pondered by both conservative and radical women. The former might learn the relation of freedom to duty, and the latter may well consider the perils which surround each onward step.... Miss Cobbe might have called her book 'Old Duties in New Lights.' It must help many women to lead sincere, self-reliant lives, and to determine at critical moments what their action shall be."—*Mrs. Elizabeth K. Churchill, in the Providence Journal.*

"The best of all books on 'Women's Duties.' Now that George Eliot is gone, there is probably no woman in England so well equipped for general literary work as Miss Cobbe."—*Col. T. Wentworth Higginson, in Woman's Journal.*

"I desire to commend it to the careful perusal of women in our own country, as a book full of timely counsel and suggestion, and to all, as a valuable contribution to the literature of ethics."—*Julia Ward Howe, in Christian Register.*

"Just now, the first 'Duty of Women' is to read this whole book with studious self-application; for it is rich in saving common sense, warm with the love of man, and consecrated by the love of God."—*Miss Harriet Ware Hall, in Unitarian Review.*

"What is best in the whole book is that she founds her teaching for women so strongly in the deepest and simplest moral principles that her thoughts come with a force and breadth which win for them at once a respectable hearing."—*London Spectator.*

"One of the notable books of the season.... No true woman can read these lectures without being stirred by them to completer life."—*Morning Star.*

"In Miss Cobbe's latest book, 'The Duties of Women,' there is much to be commended for its common sense and its helpfulness. Miss Cobbe goes down to the principles underlying the topics of which she speaks; and the strength with which she utters her thoughts is the strength of conviction and of earnest purpose."—*Sunday School Times.*

"This is the very volume needed for parents to intrust to their daughters when leaving home for school, and for earnest friends to offer young brides, as a wedding gift."

Fourth Edition. Cloth. 12mo. $1.00.
New Cheap Edition. Paper. 25 cents.

For sale by booksellers, and mailed, postpaid, on receipt of the price, by

Geo. H. Ellis, Publisher, Boston.

INSTITUTE ESSAYS:

READ BEFORE THE "MINISTERS' INSTITUTE," PROVIDENCE, R.I., OCTOBER, 1879.

CONTENTS:

INTRODUCTION,	Rev. H. W. BELLOWS.
FATHER, SON, AND HOLY GHOST,	Rev. S. R. CALTHROP.
THE RELATION OF MODERN PHILOSOPHY TO LIBERALISM,	Prof. C. C. EVERETT.
INFLUENCE OF PHILOSOPHY UPON CHRISTIANITY,	F. E. ABBOT.
MONOTHEISM AND THE JEWS,	Dr. GUSTAV GOTTHEIL.
THE IDEA OF GOD,	Rev. J. W. CHADWICK.
THE AUTHORSHIP OF THE FOURTH GOSPEL,	Prof. EZRA ABBOT.
THE GOSPEL OF JOHN,	Rev. FRANCIS TIFFANY.
METHODS OF DEALING WITH SOCIAL QUESTIONS,	Rev. J. B. HARRISON.
ETHICAL LAW AND SOCIAL ORDER,	Rev. GEO. BATCHELOR.

"To the reader of comparative theologies, this book has a special interest."—*Zion's Herald.*

"The publication of this volume is one of the great tide-marks of theological progress in the United States."—*Free Religious Index.*

"Of all the compilations to which Unitarian discussions have given rise, this will be found the most solid and meaty."—*Christian Register.*

"The cause of Unitarianism will have to take care of itself; but it is a matter of great public importance when clergymen, however stationed in practical life, address themselves without reserve and without qualification to the ascertainment of philosophic truth. How well this has been done at the Providence meeting of the 'Institute' is shown by this volume, which is entitled to the cordial attention not only of students of theology, but also of those interested in high truth. Those who know enough, and those whose religious system has been completed, had better not approach a volume which, to a seeker after fa··" 's wonderfully grateful and stimu'ating."—*Boston Advertiser.*

8vo, 280 pp. Cloth, $1.25; paper, $1.00.

THREE PHASES OF MODERN THEOLOGY:

CALVINISM, UNITARIANISM, LIBERALISM.

By JOSEPH HENRY ALLEN, A.M.,

LECTURER ON ECCLESIASTICAL HISTORY IN HARVARD UNIVERSITY.

"The addresses rest throughout on Christian theism, the ethical spirit, the temperate soul, vast reading, and good judgment. They are singularly dispassionate and well balanced, and good readers will find them healthful as well as stimulating and helpful."—*Boston Advertiser.*

8vo, 68 pp. Paper. Price 35 cents.

THE MINISTER'S HAND-BOOK,

FOR CHRISTENINGS, WEDDINGS, AND FUNERALS.

COMPILED AND ARRANGED

By Rev. MINOT J. SAVAGE.

This little volume contains a service for the baptism of children, several forms of marriage service, and a variety of burial services, with a number of selections in prose and poetry suitable for use at funerals. At the end of the book are a dozen blank pages, for such additions as individual taste may indicate. It is well printed in clear, large type, and put up in neat, flexible binding, its size and shape being arranged especially for the pocket.

Flexible cloth, 75 cents; full Turkey morocco, gilt edges, stamped with owner's name in gold, $2.50.

For sale by booksellers, or sent by mail by

Geo. H. Ellis, Publisher, 141 Franklin Street, Boston.

www.ingramcontent.com/pod-product-compliance
Lightning Source LLC
Chambersburg PA
CBHW031448160426
43195CB00010BB/902